For No Good Reason

Yosemite granite

For No Good Reason

*climbs & climbing
mountains & mountaineering*

Lito Tejada-Flores

Western Eye Press
2017

For No Good Reason
is published by
WESTERN EYE PRESS,
*a small independent publisher
(very small, and very independent) with
a home base in the Colorado Rockies
and an office in Sedona Arizona.*
For No Good Reason *is also
available as an eBook
in various formats.*

© *2017 Lito Tejada-Flores*
Western Eye Press
P O Box 1008
Sedona, Arizona 86339
1 800 333 5178
www.WesternEyePress.com

First edition, 2017
ISBN13   978-0-941283-46-5

Cover:
thinking about what's next
photo Chris Jones

Contents

Introduction: Why? — vii

ESSAYS

    Games Climbers Play — 3

    Second Thoughts on Climbing Games — 15

    Overpopulation and the Alpine Ego Trip — 21

CLIMBS

    The Crooked Road to the Far North — 27

    Fourth of July on the East Face of Mt. Morrison — 51

    With Daredevil on the Grand Traverse — 55

    Fitz Roy, The Way it Wasn't — 65

    Fromage to Patagonia — 69

FICTION

    Rojo's Peón — 75

    Who Goes Up Must Come Down — 85

Why?

LET'S GET THIS ONE OUT OF THE WAY. Not the question. It's here to stay: Why do you climb? Why did you start climbing? Why did you keep on climbing? Why do you, why does anyone, want to climb? No matter how clever Mallory's answer about Everest: "Because it's there." No matter how thoughtful, or light-hearted, the real answer is always the same: *for no good reason.*

And that's good enough. Maybe that's the whole story.

Part One

Essays

Bouldering, the purest game

Games Climbers Play

Reality is the apparent absence of contradiction
—Louis Arragon, *Le Paysan de Paris*

I

WHAT I SHOULD LIKE TO PROPOSE IN THIS ESSAY is not a new answer to the basically unanswerable question, what is climbing?, but rather a new way of talking and thinking about it. Climbing is not a homogeneous sport but rather a collection of differing (though related) activities, each with its own adepts, distinctive terrain, problems and satisfactions, and perhaps most important, its own rules. Therefore, I propose to consider climbing in general as a hierarchy of climbing-games, each defined by a set of rules and an appropriate field of play.

The word game seems to imply a sort of artificiality which is foreign to what we actually feel on a climb. The attraction of the great walls, above all, is surely that when one is climbing them one is playing 'for keeps.' Unlike the player in a bridge game, the climber cannot simply lay down his cards and go home. But this does not mean that climbing is any less a game. Although the player's actions have real and lasting consequences, the decision to start playing is just as gratuitous and unnecessary as the decision to start a game of chess. In fact, it is precisely because there is no necessity to climb that we can describe climbing as a game.

The obstacles one must surmount to gain the summit of Indian Rock in Berkeley or The Hand at Pinnacles National Monument are scarcely of the same order as those defending the West Face of Sentinel Rock in Yosemite or the North Face of the Eiger. And the personal satisfaction of the climber upon having solved each of these problems could hardly be the same. As a result, a handicap system has evolved to equalize the inherent challenge and maintain the climber's feeling of achievement at a high level in each of these different situations. This handicap system is realized through the rules of the various climbing-games.

It is important to realize at the outset that these rules are negatively expressed although their aim is positive. They are nothing more than a series of don'ts: don't use fixed ropes, belays, pitons, a series of camps, etc. The purpose of these negative rules is essentially protective or conservative. That is, they are designed to conserve the climber's feeling of personal (moral) accomplishment against the meaninglessness of a success which represents merely technological victory.

Let us take as a concrete example the most complex game in the climbing hierarchy—bouldering. It is complex by definition since it has more rules than any other climbing game, rules which prohibit nearly everything—ropes, pitons and belayers. All that is left is the individual standing in front of a rock problem. (It should be noted that an upper belay or "top-roping" belongs to practice climbing, that is, merely training for any of the real climbing-games). But why so many restrictions? Only because boulders are too accessible; they don't defend themselves well enough. For example, it would be an absurdity to use a ladder to reach the top of a boulder in Fontainbleau, the famous bouldering area outside Paris, but to use the same ladder to bridge a crevasse in the Khumbu Icefall might be reasonable since Everest defends itself so well that one ladder no longer tips the scales toward certain success. Thus the basic principle of a handicap is applied to maintain a degree of uncertainty as to the eventual outcome, and from this very uncertainty stems the adventure and personal satisfaction of climbing.

More generally, I discern a complete spectrum of climbing-games, ranked according to the complexity (or number) of their rules. The higher one goes on the scale, the more inaccessible and formidable become the climber's goals, and, in consequence, one needs apply fewer restrictions to conserve the full measure of challenge and satisfaction inherent in the climbing-game that one is playing. At the top of the hierarchy we find the expedition-game, which, although complicated to organize and play, is formalistically speaking, the simplest game of all, since virtually nothing is forbidden to the climber. The recent use of airplanes and helicopters exemplifies the total lack of rules in the pure expedition-game.

While variant games have arisen in isolated and special circumstances, and in different countries, one can distinguish the following seven basic climbing games:

1. The Bouldering Game

We have already discussed bouldering, but one should note that the basic bouldering rules eliminate not only protection but also companions. The boulderer is essentially a solo climber. In fact, when we see solo climbing at any level of difficulty it represents the application of bouldering rules to some other climbing-game. Aside from that, this game is found in every country where climbing exists, although the number of climbers who specialize in it is relatively small.

2. The Crag Climbing Game

Crag climbing as a pure game form may have reached its highest form of expression in the British Isles. It is practiced on cliffs of limited size—routes averaging one to three pitches in length. Because of their limited size and the large amount of time at the climber's disposal, such routes are not imposing enough to be approached with the full arsenal of the climber's tools (though they may contain moves as hard as those of any climb). Fundamentally the game consists in climbing them free with the use of extremely well-defined and limited protection. The use of pitons is avoided or, in special cases, standardized at an absolute minimum. Pure crag climbing is scarcely practiced as a game in this country (that is, in the US) except in areas such as Pinnacles National Monument, where the rock is virtually unpitonable. There are, however, a number of areas in the States, such as the Shawangunks in upstate New York, where the crag climbing game could be played with more rigor.

3. The Continuous Rock-Climbing Game

This is the game that most California climbers know best. It differs from the crag game in allowing the full range of rock climbing equipment to be used at the discretion of the climber as well as allowing the use of direct aid. Fundamentally this game should be played on longer, multi-pitch climbs whose length puts a kind of time limit to the mechanical means that a climber can employ and still reach the top. Shorter climbs should still be approached as more complex games with stricter rules.

4. The Big Wall Game

This game is practiced not only on the bigger Yosemite walls but in the Dolomites and elsewhere. It is characterized by the prolonged periods of time spent on the walls and by the fact that each member of the party does not have to climb every lead (e.g., different climbers may prusik with loads on different days but are still considered to have done the entire climb). The full technical and logistic equipment range is allowed. In the modern big wall game fixed ropes to the ground and multiple attempts to prepare the route are no longer allowed (see part II), and a rigorous distinction is still made between free and artificial moves and pitches.

5. The Alpine Climbing Game

In alpine climbing the player encounters for the first time the full range of hostile forces present in the mountain environment. In addition to problems of length and logistics and pure technical climbing difficulty, one meets increased objective dangers in the form of falling rock, bad weather and extreme cold, and bad conditions such as verglas. All this leads to a further relaxation of formal rules since success in the game may often include merely surviving. In alpine climbing the use of pitons is avoided wherever possible because of time loss in situations where speed means safety, but where pitons are used there is a tendency to use them as holds also. Thus the rules of this game do not require one to push all leads free. The restrictions upon the player are more determined by the nature of the mountain and the route than by a set of rules accepted in advance.

6. The Super-Alpine Game

This is the newest climbing-game to appear and is not yet completely understood. It rejects expedition techniques on terrain which would traditionally have been suitable for it. Its only restrictive rule is that the party must be self-contained. Any umbilical-like connection in the form of a series of camps, fixed ropes, etc., to a secure base is no longer permitted. This rule provides a measure of commitment that automatically increases the uncertainty of success, making victory that much more meaningful. Often the major alpine routes under extreme winter conditions provide suitable terrain for super-alpine climbs. Some of the early, classic super-alpine routes were the South Face of Aconcagua, the first winter ascent of the Eiger North Wall, and the ascent of Cerro Torre by Egger and Maestri (the reality or truth of this ascent is now widely disputed and disbelieved, but the initial claim of this ascent certainly falls into the super-alpine category even if it was a fiction).

7. The Expedition Game

I have already mentioned the lack of rules in this game, but I wish to point out that there are still differences of personal involvement on the part of the players from expedition to expedition. For example, members of the German Broad Peak expedition who packed all their own loads up the mountain were, in a sense, playing a more difficult game than the usual Himalayan expedition that moves up the mountain on the backs of its Sherpas.

It should be noted that the above ordering of climbing-games is not an attempt to say that some games are intrinsically better, harder, or more worthwhile in themselves than others. One remembers that the very purpose of the game structure is to equalize such value connotations from game to game so that the climber who plays any of these games by its proper set of rules should have a least a similar feeling of personal accomplishment. Of course, each type of game will still have its own proponents, its own classics, heroes, and myths.

The real purpose of ranking climbing games into such a hierarchy, however, it not to make judgments about a game or its players, but rather to have a useful scale against which to discuss climbing ethics, since unethical behavior involves a disregard of certain rules.

II

Within our new framework we can now clear up certain misconceptions about climbing ethics. Ethical climbing merely means respecting the set of rules of the climbing-game that one is playing. Conversely, unethical climbing occurs when a climber attempts to use a set of rules appropriate to a game higher up on the scale than the one he is actually playing (i.e.

a less restrictive set of rules). Applying this idea to the bolt controversy that has animated ethical discussions among climbers for the last several years, we can see that there is nothing unethical about bolts per se; it is merely that their use is prohibited by the rules of certain climbing-games and not by others. In certain games the question becomes meaningless for, as Bonatti points out, on a major mixed face no amount of bolts can guarantee success, whereas an excessive number will insure defeat through lack of time.

I have assumed so far that the rules for various climbing-games were fixed. Of course, this is not the case, as both the games and their rules are undergoing a constant, if slow, evolution. The central problem of climbing ethics is really the question: who makes the rules for these games? and secondarily: how do they change with time?

On reflection, it seems to me that the rules of various climbing-games are determined by the climbing community at large, but less so by climbers approaching the two extremes of ability. One of these extremes is composed of those fainthearted types who desire to overcome every new difficulty with some kind of technological means rather than at the expense of personal effort under pressure. The other group is the small nucleus of elite climbers whose basic concern is not with merely ethical climbing but with minimizing the role of technology and increasing that of individual effort in order to do climbs with better style. But before talking about style, and the role of the elite climber in climbing evolution, I want to expand my idea that the majority of climbers are responsible for deciding the rules of a given climbing-game.

No matter what their origin a set of rules must be consecrated by usage and general acceptance. Thus, the way good climbers have always done a climb becomes the traditional way of doing it; the rules become classic and constitute an ethical minimum for the climb, defining at the same time the climbing-game to which it belongs. But what of new climbs? At any moment there are relatively few members of the climbing community capable of doing significant first ascents; these will be members of the creative elite we have already mentioned. The question arises: should the style they use on a first ascent determine the rules for succeeding ascents? I think not (although their approaches and attitudes will of course serve as guidelines for following parties). Examples of cases where the first ascent has not set the pattern for succeeding ascents are almost too numerous to list. Just because Jeff Foote made the first ascent of Patio Pinnacle solo, or because Bonatti soloed the South-West Pillar of the Drus, following climbers have felt under no obligation to stick to the difficult rules of the first ascent; or just because the first ascent of the Eiger North Wall was made in a storm, no one has seriously suggested that later parties wait for bad weather to go up the face. A kind of group prudence is at work here, rejecting individual solutions whose extremism puts them beyond the reach of the majority of competent climbers climbing at any given period.

What then, is the role of the small minority of extreme climbers in the evolution of climbing-games? To understand it we must first develop the idea of climbing style. Style may be defined as the conscious choice of a set of rules for a given climbing-game. Thus, if a climber follows the accepted rules for a given game he is climbing both in classical style and ethically. Bad style and unethical climbing are synonymous, and both represent the choice of rules from a simpler (higher) game, such as alpine climbing with expedition style. On the other hand, a climber can choose to climb with "better" style, that is with rules lower down in the hierarchy than that of the climbing-game which he is playing. A fitting example would be the way John Gill has applied bouldering rules to certain crag climbing problems, doing extremely hard, unprotected moves high off the ground.

In this way the creative nucleus of elite climbers can express itself by climbing with better style than the average climber (like aristocrats playing a more demanding game than the democratic majority), which certainly provides enough room for personal expression, yet seems to avoid the traditional aristocratic role of leadership and direction. In fact, these climbers lead the majority only indirectly—their responsibility is not to determine and set ethical standards (rules) for the majority but rather to demonstrate their superior style. Thus, they stake out the possible directions for the evolution of climbing-games. And this, aside from suffering the wiles of equipment-mongers, is the only way that such changes can come about.

Let me give a concrete example. The most evident is the way in which the rules of the big-wall game have evolved in Yosemite Valley under the influence of the best climbers of the day whose primary concern was to do their own climbs in the best style possible rather than to impose an arbitrary set of rules on all climbers. After the feasibility of doing the bigger Grade VI walls without siege tactics had been consistently demonstrated, climbers were impressed enough to accept this approach as a basic rule to such an extent that today even strangers to the Yosemite climbing community (such as the two Frenchmen who climbed the Nose of El Capitan in the spring of 1966) follow it as a matter of course.

In a less dramatic way the rules of all climbing-games are changing constantly, becoming ever more restrictive in order to preserve the fundamental challenge that the climber is seeking from the inroads of a fast changing technology. The present laissez-faire of the uppermost games is disappearing slowly as the complexity of rules shifts up the spectrum. The eventual "victim," of course, will be the expedition game which will disappear completely as super-alpine climbing takes its place. This is not only the newest but, in a sense, the most creative climbing-game, since here the nature of the obstacles encountered is so severe that it will be a long, long time before technological advances even begin to encroach upon the climber's personal satisfaction. The possibilities, on the other hand, are immense. One can even visualize the day when, with ultra-modern bivouac gear, a climbing party of two sets off to do an 8000m peak just as today one sets off to do a hard route on the Grand Teton or on Mont Blanc.

Here, I think, this essay should end. Not because speculations about the future of climbing are either futile or uninteresting, but because we have already wandered far enough from our original subject. That climbing will continue to evolve is a certainty, although it is far less certain that the idea of climbing-games is the best basis for looking at this evolution. But surely this, or any, new framework for thinking and talking about what we are actually doing when we climb is at least a valid step toward the future.

Ascent magazine 1967

Learning lesssons in the Alps, direct west face Aguille du Dru

Alpinism as Humanism

Second Thoughts on Climbing Games

CLIMBING: AN ARBITRARY GAME, played for keeps. Not so serious, yet very serious indeed. For real, but not quite real. A self-imposed set of rules, restrictions, and personal roadblocks thrown up on a road to nowhere, that is to say anywhere and everywhere: Start here, at the base of this rock, this slab, this crack—the infamous Point A—and finish up there, on top of that boulder, that ledge, that peak—the mythical Point B.

Call it a route, call it a climb, call it a game, because you and your friends made up the rules and (mostly) obeyed them, because how you got there was more important than just getting there, because really we're only playing (aren't we?), not climbing *for* something, or *to* something, or with something else in mind. Instead of pursuing goals too easily reached, we were.... what? Embracing the now? The now or never? Measuring meaning by a finely tuned balance of natural and self-imposed challenges—the harder the climb and the less likely our success, the fewer rules we needed to preserve that inner adrenaline rush of uncertainty, the doubt essential to adventure. And vice versa: The easier the goal, the more radical and restrictive were the rules we'd choose.

That's more or less the way I put it when I wrote "Games Climbers Play" some twenty-odd years ago, a kind of pre-postmodern analysis of climbing as an intense, elegant, arbitrary game, an analysis that has stood up pretty well over time. A nice idea, more or less true. Seems I was right. And also wrong. Climbing, it has slowly dawned on me, is often both less and more than just a game.

Less what? Well, a hell of a lot less pure, for one thing. The beauty, it always seemed to me, of treating climbing as a game was the delicious pointlessness of it all, the arbitrary commitment of time, energy, strength, talent, cunning, and courage to a task that really didn't need to be done. The act of climbing was its own definition, its own reason and motivation, a self-justifying feedback loop that never looked outside itself to society for validation.

A rather "sixties" idea, it now strikes me: the sense that when you climbed you stopped, literally, everything else. Because if the climb was demanding enough, if you'd understood the game and sharpened the rules to that perfect pitch, then you wouldn't have room in your consciousness for anything else. Your universe would both shrink and expand to the next hold, the next few feet of face, the next phase of this empty-in-advance safe you were cracking, hidden combination by hidden combination, for its own sake, empty of everything but the challenge accepted, the problem solved.

Yeah, sure, sometimes it worked that way, and often it still does. Sometimes we do leave the shit behind; the world out there gets less and less real as the rock or the ice gets more and more real. Sometimes it all drops away—school and jobs and careers and greed and ambition and relations and your sick parents, your plans for next weekend, those unpaid bills, the unchanged oil in the pickup—it all drops away and disappears before you're ten feet off the deck.

But sometimes, of course, it doesn't work out like that. Sometimes the rest of your life follows you up the crag like an endless haul line clipped to your harness, heavier and heavier each pitch. You know what I mean. One thing seems certain, climbing isn't—and never was—as pure and arbitrary a game as the simplified view I staked out in "Games Climbers Play."

Climbing, most of us agree, is a creative act. But what climbers create are not just routes, not just aesthetic statements, dotted lines up cliffs, articles in *Climbing* or *Mountain*, or footnotes in a guidebook. Climbers are busy creating their own personas and personalities, their own lives, as they climb. And when the climb is over, those lives go on, go forward: a one-way trip with no possibility of backtracking to rub out something that no longer feels quite right, looks quite right. How you climb today very soon becomes how you have climbed, which, just as rapidly, becomes who you are. In a recent Woody Allen film, a character says, "The sum of the choices you make is who you are." Not comedy this time, but fact.

The fact I'm leading up to is this: Many, maybe most of the choices climbers make (and certainly their most important choices) don't concern rock and ice and holds and dynamic moves and rope management and protection; they concern other people—climbing partners, friends, family, the community at large. Even the solo climber has made some major statements about other people, and is acting them out. These are the decisions that stick with you, define you, have long and lasting consequences. Climbing games, it turns out, always involve more than one player.

Consider two (extreme) examples: A few years ago, the cover of a Diamond-C equipment catalog carried a chilling blurb as a sort of endorsement for ice tools: It was the text of a postcard from a Japanese climber describing a solo summit dash on K2. He told of racing to the summit while another member of the party, a "young" guy not even given the dignity of a name, tries in vain to catch up and falls to his death. No regrets, no sorrow, no human connection to a fellow member of the expedition, almost no notice except that the fatal accident gave the summit day more drama. A young alpine-stud on the way up: fame, sponsorship and big-time endorsements looming large ahead.

Contrast this with another mountain drama. A French alpinist friend of mine from the 1960s and his exhausted partner were pinned down by bad weather near the summit of Mont Blanc after a winter ascent on a big south-face route. Bad judgment no doubt, over-extended and probably under-prepared. My friend, "*petit* Claude," found himself stuck in one of those situations where one's decisions really do define an entire life. He could abandon his exhausted and disoriented buddy near the summit and descend to safe haven at the Vallot Hut; he would certainly make it, his partner would certainly die. Or he could stay with him, keep him warm, take care of him as best he could and maybe, just maybe, the weather would break and they'd be rescued. A long shot that didn't work. They both died. I (and a lot of other people) lost a great friend to that storm. But thinking about it, it seems to me that *petit* Claude's life was one of those rare ones that's good to the very end. His choice on top of Mont Blanc confirmed a lot about his character, and reinforced all our reasons for loving and admiring him.

Is this an unfair comparison? To say that one climber died affirming life (a failure that was really a success), while another made a hot climb while turning his back on life (a success that was an appalling and stupid failure)? I don't think so. My point is that while climbing games themselves are both arbitrary and asocial (there simply is no real reason to climb other than "because...."), climbers also function in a broader context, in a world shared with others—a world where we define ourselves by the way our private games, ambitions, and dreams interact with those of other people. Climbers escape many but not all judgments. The meaning of a climb, any climb, is always twofold: There is the meaning we draw directly from challenge, movement, and skill, but also a meaning that depends on how (or whether) the climber's actions will affect others. The same climb, for example, can be both very hard and very commercial. A climb can be admirable in one sense and contemptible in another. It can sometimes, in fact, be absolutely value-neutral to anyone but the climber, yet I'd say that's rather rare. It is hardly surprising that climbers, instead of climbing out of the complex web of daily life into something like solitude, discover that the radical nature of their choices while climbing lead to radical consequences in other people's lives as well as their own. Climbing is no exit from the dense tangled ecology of intentions and results we also call life.

The idea of climbing games has proved a strong one, but not strong enough to block out the larger context or consequences of climbing. I wish I could just assert that, in addition to being a fascinating complex of games, alpinism is also a form of humanism. Today, unfortunately, it's not that clear.

First published in the Fall 1990 issue of Summit magazine.

....the charm of uncrowded routes....

Overpopulation & the Alpine Ego Trip

WE LIVE IN AN AGE OF CONCERN. Concern generated by ever-accelerating changes in our environment—technological, social, psychological—and our own difficulty in responding. Values crumble and are swept away, others resist erosion, and new ones are formed. Almost blindly, individuals continue to cling to their set idea of the good, and resist whatever threatens it.

This sense of concern is very much present in the climbing community today*. It animates climbers' talk and spills onto the pages of their magazines (see The End of the Mountains by Chris Jones, The Last of the Mountain Men by Jim McCarthy, and Yvon Chouinard's piece in this issue of *Ascent*). Though there is a new awareness that all is not well with climbing, the general complaint seems to be a paraphrase of François Villon's fifteenth-century lament: *Où sont les neiges d'antan?* Where are the snows (read: values) of yesteryear?" The source of our nebulous but very real malaise is invariably found in numbers: there are too many of us now (read: there are too many of them doing what was once our thing). Overpopulate the mountains, runs the general consensus, and you destroy the mountain experience.

I disagree! Both with the idea and on specific points. Are the mountains really overcrowded now? I submit that only at two ends of the mountain spectrum do we see overcrowding. At the creative-elitist end, of course, there are too many people nowadays. Frankly, if you want

---

* *Today, in this case, was 1972*

to be a hero, it's not that easy any more. First ascents no longer come cheap. Near major population centers one must be a fantastic climber, not merely a good one, to reap the ego-gratification of getting there first. Otherwise it's the long, troublesome pilgrimage to the remote ranges. And even then, who knows if you'll be first (with all those others nowadays), and who knows if it still means as much? Making a first ascent today doesn't imply that you are as unique a human being as it formerly did. Hard times for ego freaks, that's for sure!

At the other end of the spectrum, we have the "sheep-following-the-leader" syndrome, the phenomenon of the "popular" route, and the detestable queuing-up at the foot of a climb. This is overcrowding at its worst, but luckily, its social nature confines it to relatively few climbs, in relatively few mountain areas. People simply do not swarm all over the crags in all directions, but rather follow each other in patient lines up one or two climbs that are the current ones to do. Examples are legion. In Yosemite, the South Face of the Column is a dirty thoroughfare, but Sentinel and Quarter Domes, not *à la mode*, are shadowy and deserted. In the Tetons, there is always traffic on the famous North Face of the Grand, but the West Face, a better climb, is left silent and alone. In Chamonix, the Walker Spur of the Grandes Jorasses has seen well over a hundred ascents, while the beautiful Central Spur has been climbed less than twenty times, and two other routes on the same face have never been repeated. The sad truth is that a few climbs (but very few) have been sacrificed on the twin altars of publicity and populism.

Our lamentations, however, are premature. Let's look between the limiting parentheses of high-powered competitive climbing on the one hand, and the essentially mindless ticking off of classic, popular routes on the other, and try to see what's left. Fortunately, quite a lot. Quantitatively and qualitatively, the great majority of routes, mountains and mountain areas, as well as the major part of the mountain experience, remains unscathed—still far from the madding crowd, oblivious to and safe from the population pressures at either extreme. If one isn't trying to get one's name into a guidebook, if one is willing to take the trouble of figuring out one's own climbing program instead of doing only the routes one's friends did last summer, then the mountains and the crags will suddenly seem as uncrowded as they must have seemed to David Brower's generation, thirty years ago.

The period we are now living through is not the end of the mountains, but it is the end of a certain style of mountaineering. Although this style produced an enormous number of hard climbs, we can still call it *l'alpinisme de facilité*, or simplistic, facile mountaineering. Me-firstism, or just climbing what everyone else climbs—these are psychologically simple, almost lazy, ways of behaving, an unthinking frontier approach now passing into extinction. From now on, a wilderness experience will have to be created, not simply indulged in. It will mean more than just leaving the city. One will have to put aside certain "city" patterns that have too long accompanied us to the mountains: social patterns of obedience to the group and mass conditioning, or individual patterns of status-driven competition, whether the struggle for ego-reinforcement or the desire to belong to an elite.

These arguments may sound far-fetched, or give the impression that their author is fundamentally indifferent to the fate of mountains and mountaineering. Not so! I too share the general sense of concern that is the sign of our times. I too am distressed by certain changes in the mountain landscape, external and internal. But the conclusions I've arrived at are, I think, encouraging. My ultimate conclusion is that a real wilderness experience is the sharing of wilderness with other people, not using it to escape them. (That, however, is the subject of a different discussion.) In the meantime, I suggest that we take a new look at the mountains by first looking at how and why we climb. I suggest that the mountains are not overcrowded, but that mountaineers have not been sufficiently 'spaced out,' neither sufficiently free nor sufficiently aware. I suggest that there is a simple answer to François Villon's question: "Where are the snows of yesteryear?" They're still falling.

Part Two

Climbs

The Devil's Thumb

The Crooked Road to the Far North

I

AT A BEER GARDEN IN BERKELEY, putting down a pint with my old friend, Chris Jones, the subject of summer climbing trips came up, and that's how I got back on the road.... Chris had planned a mini-expedition to the Devil's Thumb, a redoubtable granite spire in Southeastern Alaska, with two Salt Lake City climbers, George and Jeff Lowe. Something had come up, Jeff couldn't go. Did I want to come? Sure.

The juke box was blaring out Elton John, the air warm with summer and tasty with pizza smells, students and freaks and half-naked chicks swirled around us, through the open patio, the pop-corn machine was spitting and the avant-garde cinema beside us disgorged its Fellini-eyed crowd into the night.... Not exactly an atmosphere for reflection but perhaps 'up there' would be more real than 'down here.' Sure. We left La Val's drunk and enthusiastic. Chris and George would drive most of the way, via Salt Lake and Canada, as far as Prince Rupert. I would go by bus to Seattle, then ferry boat to Petersburg, Alaska, and meet them there. We'd fly into our mountain, air-drop our gear, and climb it, even if it took us a month....

We were laughing and joking and it wasn't really too clear just what I was getting into. (On a last-minute practice climb before leaving I discovered how out of shape I was, and a real anxiety about the climb began to build up inside me.) But one thing was sure: before I knew it, I'd be traveling again, stepping out, in the grip of strange currents again, and it felt good.

> So it's starting again:
> Once more, the mad
> last-minute dash,
> hastily packed bags,
> smokey white tiles of
> Greyhound waiting rooms.
> Once more, the motives
> are uncertain & the means
> confused with the ends. Only
> the need to go (but where?)
> to do (but what?) to feel
> again (but why?) is real.
> So it's starting again:
> Once more, my mind overflows
> with debris from the future,
> with scraps from the past:
> sleepless nights, narrow seats,
> wide country, endless roads....
> Somewhere in the far north
> a mountain will do for a goal:
> And perhaps this time
> the crooked road
> will lead me straight,
> instead of sending me off
> again in search of myself,
> starting again & again....

Early in the morning in Seattle, bleary-eyed and loaded-down with ragged old duffle bags, I find my way down to Pier 48. False front of wood and plastic, giant indian totem designs, yellow and blue Alaska Marine Highway signs. Right away, I've got a problem: the list of walk-on passengers is full, closed. No, we don't make reservations but all these folks came in yesterday; first time it's ever; we'll put your name on the stand-by list; yes, we'll know around 3 or 4 this afternoon. A helluva note. Only one boat a week from Seattle, and my friends up there waiting. Screwed. Well, what can I do but trust my Karma, again and always? Leave my pack and bags at the feet of a giant stuffed Kodiak bear in the waiting room, and go out to see Seattle. .

After an endless walk in cowboy boots, I decide to eat lunch at The Prague, a gallery/restaurant in a waterfront district of run-down brick buildings, slowly being remodeled into a funky-posh shopping area. I know it's overpriced but shrug my shoulders: there won't be anything like this up north....

> Prague or Seattle, it's all the same,
> only the mind travels.... only the feeling
> that something is about to happen (or
> just has or is, right now, around
> the corner) counts. Why search for
> Gothic images here? Steinbrüke or Golem?
> A skid-row panhandler meets me at the door
> & dust-mote light pours down green vines,
> shines the wooden floor, dusts old brick walls,
> starkly hung with post-Klee prints:
> this is post-Kafka Prague, post-Dubček too.
> Only the mind travels.... Beside my soup
> spotlights hit exploded heads, magic wheels,
> spikey suns & transcendental paddle boats
> gliding through intaglio seas of scratchy green:
> horses & priests, life & death & sex,

safely under glass frames from West Germany.
Waitresses without breasts shuffle by
on 3-inch cork heels.... Only the mind travels!

Lunch is good: watermelon and fruit, cold meat and cheese, a mysterious central European soup to go with the tangled images on the wall. It's 2 o'clock. Time to say goodbye to Kafka and Klee, Teleman and Bach on the stereo, time to say goodbye to Prague and Seattle and, somehow, get on that boat to Alaska.

Back in the ferry terminal, the situation has deteriorated: there are now some 90 frustrated, confused people on the stand-by list (and a few really angry ones). Their story is the same: we telephoned from Tucson; drove all the way from L.A.; no plane till Wednesday; they promised; I told my husband, planned this trip for three months; they'll tell us at 4, no, at 5.

In the middle of this displaced-persons atmosphere is a lovely slender girl, tallish, in faded jeans and a big, loose Levi jacket. How do we begin talking? An unimportant, impersonal remark addressed at random to the milling crowd. A minute later she is saying, with a smile: Want to hitch-hike north with me if we don't get on? Inside me a small voice is already shouting yes, *yes!* I am surprised at myself. She has a little child and an enormous duffle bag. We compare luggage, miles, laugh at the impossibility of it. Don't worry, we'll get on!... A long conversation begins. Something else has begun.

Her daughter's name is Ajila: a lovely smiling face, a snub turned-up nose, short blond pigtails. She sits between us on the high ticket counter and draws with a ball-point pen on application forms for Master Charge cards.... We exchange names, fascinating bits of information that unfold and unfold: Kathleen, unlike her daughter, has dark wavy hair pulled way back, a pale oval face with only two spots of color on her cheeks, prominent without being really high-boned. A tiny gold dot in a pierced nostril makes me think of gypsies, central Europe, far away places.

She is beautiful without being beautiful. She doesn't sparkle, she glows. But she's real, she's tired, has real problems, a real mixed-up past, her own crooked road leading her north. She's going to Ketchikan to meet her old man, they'll travel, work, she's not sure, maybe she'll wind up working as a nurse as she did in Crescent City.... Her dreams are close to the surface: she talks about going to South America someday, adopting a lot of kids.... Ajila? It's supposed to be an Arabic name, her father studied Arabic, no, someone else, she married him to keep him out of the Army....

Around us people fester and complain. Behind the counter, the harassed clerks with their gold and blue ALASKA HOST pins pretend not to notice the people on the other side. But eventually the purser's list arrives with 96 free places: room for everyone, I think. My own name is third on the list. I buy my ticket and stagger to the gangplank under my enormous bags.

The M.V. Malaspina is so big that its levels, decks and passageways seem, at first, a labyrinth. I lug my duffle bags in relays to the solarium on the top rear deck of the big blue and white boat. This is home. What next? Look for Kathleen, of course. I meet her at the top of the stairway from the car deck; her bags are down there, so we go down again and I carry them up on the deck. We're still amazed at having got on board at all. And we sit down, out of breath, and stare at Seattle, rising up the hill behind the waterfront in grey tiers of freeways and office buildings, a grey city under a cloudy sky. It looks like rain.

We relax, the three of us, on a wooden box-seat full of life preservers, peeling oranges while Kathleen makes cheese sandwiches from the food left in her old carpet bag. A bushy-whiskered, prophet-like figure of a man walks by (prospector? recluse? hermit?) dressed in Army fatigue pants and an old brown sweat shirt. Are you hungry? Would you like some? Kathleen knows, offers, dispenses, smiles. Strange easy-going vibes are all around her, all around us.

Paul is, indeed, an old recluse with a philosophical bent, going up to

Wrangell to "work in the woods." He takes me down to the deck below to show me a part of the ship he has "captured," hanging a large blue and orange tarp across a corner of the covered walkway. Beneath it are his incredibly worn-looking possessions and his pride and joy, a big black iron pot. He pulls two beers from a paper bag. One for your wife. No, she's only my friend. A strange rush of emotion that will be explained later, or never.

When we get back to the solarium, the ship is just casting off; silently, imperceptibly at, first, the long wharves slide away from us, gathering momentum as the whole panorama of Seattle distorts, expands, recedes. ... It takes a long time to lose the city astern, but already we're in a new space. The North is already more real, our day-to-day lives-already half-forgotten. Under threatening skies we enter another world:

>Bluegreen water
>>beside
>
>Greygreen forests
>>beneath
>
>Yellowgrey clouds,
>>thru
>
>The sundeck roof
>>where
>
>Raindrops dance
>>on the grey
>
>Plexiglass windows
>>& the grey
>
>Velvet fabric
>>of dreams.

The solarium is full of backpackers, young people, freaks. Kelty packs and down sleeping bags are everywhere. Paul spreads a hundred-year old, hand-embroidered quilt on a kind of raised dias, like a legendary bearded pasha out of the Arabian Nights. Down inside the boat, there is a second scramble for the remaining staterooms. The other walk-on passengers, those of a certain age, or a certain life-style, will be spending the night stiffly upright in airplane-type lounge chairs. They don't look very comfortable, or very happy....

The evening is forever. Already the northern latitude gives us more daylight than we're used to. It's a late long twilight, the lamps are on, Kathleen and Ajila are tucked under a forest-green sleeping bag. I lie on my stomach on deck chair beside her, and we talk, ask, answer, tell: What kind of women do you get involved with? A funny question, women like you. (My words surprise me, the feeling doesn't.)

Our talk takes us back to our other lives, takes us forward to the edge of the Far North, the edge of our own dreams. We surprise each other by talking of death, finding that we've both met it, thought about it, made a temporary truce with it. Kathleen has put a degree of order into a confused life.

She talks of her "life plan," a good one if slightly impossible, as anything must be that makes sense. She asks me questions that stop my standard answers cold. Her face is full of possible answers. Her beauty is as hard to understand as my reasons for taking this trip, or wanting to climb that mountain. I fall asleep beside her with an open heart.

Tomorrow we'll wake up to the same gentle motion, the same heavy clouds, anonymous forest channels moving mysteriously past.

> The boat glides on and on
> shedding an outworn skin of
> miles behind it while I too
> wriggle painfully forward
> out of my own past
> leaving the transparent scales
> of a hot California summer
> shimmering in the wake....

> And so we drift North
> through the fog,
> toward a second summer
> and a new skin.

The next day was long and lazy, monotonously beautiful, and at the same time full of a quiet excitement that had nothing to do with the scenery —the low forested hills sliding by on either side, the stark rocky inlets, isolated homesteads, tiny lighthouses, lonely channel markers on a lost spit of granite, sudden waterfalls cascading out of the clouds into the inky blue of the strait.

We walked and read, and even ventured into the high-priced world of the ship's cafeteria for coffee and hot chocolate for Ajila. We met our fellow vagabonds on the rear deck, and talked about their trips, and their scenes. The real landscape of people and faces began to take shape. There were climbing boots to grease and free hot showers to enjoy, and the lazy quiet flow of water on every side to pace us through the day. In the evening I wrote a small poem for Kathleen and gave it to her:

> Frontiers are places so beautiful,
> and so empty, that men
> have to fill them with dreams.
> Frontier women, too, have
> calm deep faces that
> make men dream....
> It's good to know that
> both still exist,
> and that you're
> one.

Her smiles went through me like knives. Wherever she went on board, the, air would ripple around her. I enjoyed watching her random movement on our deckside world: finding her and losing her, smiling, exchanging private glances, watching her disappear around a bulkhead, spotting her through a window, noticing how other people were attracted into her orbit, coming up to her to offer their smiles, their gifts, listening to Ajila play with the other kids on board, only smiling when I noticed that her mother wasn't really as beautiful as she seemed to be.... Her beauty was beneath and behind beauty. I was in love with a gentle dark-haired puzzle in faded blue jeans.

Everyone in the solarium that evening looked hungry. In any case, no one could afford to eat in the cafeteria, much less the dining room. The prices were unbelievable. Someone, I think one of the kids on a bicycle trip from Seattle, suggested pooling our food for a community dinner. (Some hadn't thought to go shopping before our departure, and others, caught in the 'stand-by list,' hadn't had time.) It was a huge success, a feast, not a dinner. Food appeared from everywhere: bread, cheese, sardines, celery, fruit, peanut butter, cold meats, cookies.... I bought some Rainier beer and Jay, the neuro-psychologist whose daughter played with Ajila, contributed some wine. We were already drunk without it. Serious bearded faces, young hairless ones, homely girls beginning to look pretty because they were having such a good time. Paul was there, beaming like a prophet; and the art-school teacher from the east coast who had sketched Kathleen resting against her duffel bag; two teen-aged boys from Maine who looked as if they hadn't eaten for days; pint-sized touselheaded Ray, a diminutive chain-smoking 16 year-old whose dad was a steward on the ferry, on his way back to Alaska after a year in an "institution" for some adolescent craziness, smiling and stuffing his face like the rest of us. Ajila was kneeling at her mother's side. Incongruously, older 'straight' people were drawn into the warm circle of our picnic on the floating bank of this endless winding ocean highway.

After dinner we borrowed the ship's vacuum for our crumbs, then played charades till midnight, laughing, jumping up, crying out, losing track again and again, still drunk with each other, coming down slowly,

slowly, like the long pale northern evening, reluctant to give up the last light in the sky, or in each other's faces....

Fatigue finally triumphed. The kids were already asleep. Ajila was a blond Moslem angel under her green nylon sleeping bag. Lounge chairs were pulled out flat to sleep on. Kathleen and I headed below decks for a midnight drink in the ship's bar. A perfect day, perfect evening. I wanted to stretch it out, talk to her until the words dried up, until there was nothing left to say—knowing that in a life you hardly begin, that one more evening wasn't even time to begin....

In the bar we talked, drank Scotch because neither of us could think of anything else to order, listened to a guy in the booth across the way thump out a bluegrass polka on his banjo, laughed when two of the cyclists from Washington, brother and sister, started to dance crazily up and down the narrow aisle. Out of breath from dancing, Mike came over to sit with us: his hair sticking out in all directions, his chambray shirt pulled out, his thick smiling lips covered with fever blisters (beautiful people, we learn, don't have to be too beautiful). And out of the blue, he delivered a crazy, moving, totally disarming speech about Kathleen and me, about having watched us on the ship, about the way we stayed together without grabbing onto each other, about watching the way Kathleen treated her little girl with such respect, letting her choose what to do next, what clothes to wear in the morning.... And going on to talk about himself, his efforts to find himself, not to be possessive with girlfriends, with people.... And he said a lot more, but what moved us was how he said it. Letting the barrier between himself, his ego and his words become eggshell-thin, exposing himself in a strange trusting way to talk to us like that, so that we learned more from where the words were coming than from the words themselves. At any rate, we blushed when he talked about the two of us, but he was right: our bond in the present was so real we hadn't even begun to hold onto each other for an imaginary tomorrow. Even the bar was closing, we left.

There you are. Happiness, desire, perfection. Where, if not inside you? Who, if not us now? When, if not here now? We fell asleep, warm on the cold deck, arms outside our sleeping bags, hands clasped.

REBORN under dazzling blue skies. They stole the clouds during the night. Nothing to do. A million things to do. Time rushes forward out of control. Before we can adjust, Ketchikan is swimming into view like a postcard of some far Norwegian village. The dark blue water is full of pale white jelly-fish. At the railing, Ajila has a tearful moment, imagining that we'll have to swim ashore. No, it's not like that at all. Minutes later I'm carrying their duffle bag downstairs and across the ramp to Ketchikan. Farewell is a little picnic on the rocky bank, a few words, Ajila crying out: Oh, mommy, you kissed him! and an incredible knot of emotions in my stomach. Kathleen's old man, the fellow she's been living with for two years, should be arriving on the afternoon ferry from the north, and the three of them will have to begin the business of making a new life. All my concern, my good wishes, for her, for them, seem superfluous; of course, it will work.

Back on board, I remember my Solzhenitsyn novel, *The Cancer Ward*, that she was reading, find it in my pack and manage to run ashore at the very last minute to give it to her. An extra farewell, stolen kisses. Kathleen and Ajila running out to the dock's end as the Malaspina pulls slowly away. My eyes are full of tears. I've just lived through something unbelievable. Paul is standing beside me at the rail. Whatever he is saying seems to make sense, with such a long grey beard he must have lived through all this too.... The knot in my stomach starts to untie itself, we're still moving north.

Back on the top deck I find my friends the bicycle-campers and a few others sitting around in shorts and cut-offs, having (in the simplest possible way, and so unself-consciously) a kind of Quaker-like Sunday-morning communion, sharing a giant chunk of rye-crisp, taking a few moments to think about it and share their thoughts.

> Breaking bread
> with brothers and sisters
> sitting in sunshine
> sharing white wine
> sharing our weakness
> warm in the sunshine
> feeling our strength
> not yours not mine
> quiet communion
> on a grey steel deck
> taking our turns
> talking of love
> listening by turns
> to brother and sister
> sitting in sunshine
> breaking bread.

Everything that's happened so far has made us all high, and that's the way it stays, all day. Paul leaves us at Wrangell, the next port, with his incredible collection of surplus equipment and his beautiful antique quilt. Hot-rodding teenagers are driving motor boats through the pilings of the pier, and one runs headlong into a cement footing, flips 20 feet into the water and emerges unhurt. A carnival atmosphere with everything but flags fluttering in the breeze. But the magnet keeps pulling us, we keep on moving North.

> Perhaps this is the Far North:
> The water opens and islands
> pull back their forest tongues
> for us to pass.... Overhead
> black and white clouds are fighting
> their ancient Taoist battle

> (summer's victory a fragile truce).
> In the distance now, rain streaks
> are staining the pale sky with rust.
> White mountains rear up, like
> welcoming ghosts or new friends
> on the far edge of our dreams.
> Wrangell Narrows swallows our boat.
> Rainbows welcome us to the Far North.

Time to repack my bags. We're almost to Petersburg. The northern sunset has just begun in a high-contrast battle of burnished gold and inky blue. Someone says: Look, your mountain! Yes, there it is all right, even though it isn't mine. The incredible Devil's Thumb, even this far away, it's overwhelming! I wonder how we'll ever find the courage to climb it, but I know we will. It always feels like this. Kevin, one of the cyclists gives me a small card, a poem that a friend had written for him a long time ago. Here, take this, for the summit ...

> "It's the time you have
> wasted for your rose
> that makes it so important"

Thank you. Thanks for everything. It seems impossible that I'll ever forget all this: today, this evening, these people, Kathleen and Ajila, reading poetry on the rear deck, sharing our food, such perfect uncomplicated love. I didn't come North to find this, I have almost forgotten why I came, what was behind it all, luring me up here.

> Behind snowy coastal ranges,
> behind the cobalt blue
> of Fredrick Sound evening,
> the crackerbox waterfront

of smalltown Petersburg,
behind all this there's only
a granite dream at sunset,
too icy perfect to believe in
but just real enough
to pull me off this boat....
And all our island friendship
and ferryboat love
becomes one last shout
from ship to shore
and back....
I gather up the echoes
in my rucksack
and promise myself
to spread them around,
promise to pass them on....

II

IN LITERATURE THINGS END. Stories end. Poems end. But in real life (as they say) things and people and events go on and on, world without end, forever and ever, amen. In real life you never reach the end of the crooked road. In real life there is always a part two.

For of course, getting there is only a part of the story. There one is, there you are, here I am, but yet not completely here. I'm still traveling, or else a part of me has already moved on, and ultimately I'll look back to realize that I left without ever completely arriving.... And the Far North is no different. The Far North: dream image, typewriter cliche, dimestore poetry, five-and-dime metaphysics.

But I did get here. What now? What next? Now that I'm back

in charge of my own life, at least temporarily, at least partially?... The present is Petersburg. The immediate future is the mountain, lonely and frightening on the horizon, really a thumb-like Thumb—poking up into an 11 P.M. sunset or hidden in rain and clouds, but still waiting. And the far and future future? Out there somewhere, behind the Devils's Thumb and those long snowy ridges, invisible guesswork.

Things change, time is no longer a slow crystal river.

But there are still new friends, events, poems:

>This is the calm before the storm:
>an extra day, waiting for friends,
>down by the public float, where
>spikey boats thrust long trolling poles
>up into the low clouds. The seiners
>are coming home tonight, the tenders
>will be here in an hour, and the girls
>who work in the egg room
>are having one last cup of coffee
>before reporting to their Japanese foremen.
>
>Alaskan summer: reflections in green water
>a simple life (here too, brothers and sisters)
>the circus scene of snow and trees and boats.
>Hippies migrating north for cannery jobs
>have come to civilize this hard wet land
>with their gentle talk and long wavy hair.
>
>Even the clouds look friendly now,
>and the next cloudburst, when it comes,
>will only lay more dust in my heart.
>A float-plane takes off with a roar,
>buzz saws whine, below my feet

an old hull is being scraped on the grid,
overhead: eagles, gulls, giant ravens
circle together, scream, fight and wait.
The sunshine is supercharged with mist
and the clouds are shot full of holes,
torn by sundrop, scattered by rainbeam.

I'm soaked to the skin and don't care.
Surely, this is the storm before the calm.
Afterwards will be time enough
to grab a paintbrush, tear fish from nets,
finish this life or start a new one.
This must really be the Far North,
and from here the only way is down,
all roads lead back to the world,
lead south and home.... Yes, surely,
this is the storm before the calm.

It passes quickly. It takes forever. The people of Petersburg are my clock. It's always raining, it's always cloudy, the mountain has disappeared for good. I am happy here and at peace.

The telegram reads: CAR PROBLEM ARRIVE FRIDAY EVENING PLEASE GET BATTERY CHRIS CALGARY ALBERTA. So I have an extra week to wait. I can wait. Secretly I hope they never get here, I know they will. And sure enough, when they do, a whole lifetime has passed, the rain stops, the clouds lift enough for us to fly in, drop our gear, land at the lake. And we're right on schedule again, the real schedule.

The weather keeps improving, luring us on in two days over a high pass toward the Devil's Thumb. Chris Jones, my old mate from Fitz Roy, lean and cunning, witty and optimistic. George Lowe, old friend but new companion, smiling tousle-headed physicist, full of power and quiet strength. Me and my doubts, still glad to be here, glad that it's started, that it's happening to me, this incredible scene: the ice and granite battlefield of the Witches' Cauldron, the spire-like satellite peaks, the overwhelming bulk of the Thumb itself, this mad adventure unfolding.

The weather gets better and better. Two days of rough packing to Base Camp. Collecting our flourescent orange air-drop boxes, strung out across the glacier. Dazzling white snow, dazzling blue sky, hard-edged sunshine. There will be no rest day tomorrow. Such weather is too good and too rare to waste. We have to start tomorrow and scramble to get ready. The Thumb towers overhead.

> Magic mountain—
> in all probability
> we are enchanted
> & not the mountain.
> Let's hope this magic
> pulling us up there
> will bring us down
> again.

It takes us a day and a half of snow staggering, steep step kicking and threading through unstable ice cliffs to reach the base of the rock on the south face. Our first bivouac on the snowfield ends in light rain, but morning sets things right; on we go....

The rock begins tricky, stays tricky: slantwise traversing pitches, awkward leading, awkward hauling, awkward following. George and Chris are full of fire and energy, but still they move up oh-so-slowly. At the bottom of such a great granite face, I feel—as I must have known I would—overwhelmed by the situation. A voice inside me is saying this is no place to get in shape for hard climbing, and today I manage to lead only one pitch; it will be my only real lead of the climb. Uncomfortable about contributing so little to the pointed end of the rope, I knock myself out trying to clean the pitches fast and efficiently. We do six or seven pitches, gaining the shattered diagonal ramp system that leads up across the face. A square turret-like buttress does for a bivouac platform. We're in the clouds now. The Thumb is claiming us for its own.

The next day takes us on up into the clouds, into the upper face, even into the long final summit dihedral, but also into the rain. Only a drizzle at first, but it doesn't feel healthy. It's almost midnight when Chris rappels back down out of the mist after fixing two more rope lengths above our ledge. We have an impossible time wriggling into our sleeping bags in the dark, everything wet, boots still on, eating a small snack, shouting across to George on a ledge 30 feet away, trying to sleep sitting up on our miniature ledge, fumbling with our anchor slings, waiting for dawn.

> Ice cliffs crack & groan:
> huddled on a tiny ledge,
> damp climbers moan & dream
> of warmer places, or
> lovers' faces that seem just
> out of reach, & each one
> wonders why he came
> & how long it will last.
> In the night
> enormous sheets of mist
> & rain blow slowly past.

New morning: drizzling first, then rain, then snow, whipping along in the wind, fat wet snowflakes. George and Chris are cold and wet, but still optimistic. They look up, push on back up last night's fixed ropes.

This is the low point of my climb: alone with the hauling bag and a giant wet pack, I feel sick, weak, lost. It's really snowing now. The rock is turning white. My friends are out of sight, somewhere above. For a minute I find the voice to question our judgement in going on under such deteriorating conditions, but George calls down that everything's OK. What can I do? Push off the ledge, pendulum across and start prusiking up the long thin 9mm rope. Part way up, I feel my tail rope jammed behind me, back across the traverse. I have to jumar down and back across to free the rope. I want to cry or curse. or hit something out of frustration, but save my strength for going back up....

An incredible day: everything goes slowly, awkwardly. Our dihedral world, our long vertical rock corner is half white with snow, wind begins to whistle up the slot. Near disasters follow each other like desperate warnings shouted in vain at the deaf and dumb.

I reach a tiny belay ledge, and reach out to steady myself against our big hauling bag. It starts to topple slowly off the ledge—my god! The knot in the tie-in sling has come undone. I only just barely catch it. All our food, sleeping bags, everything, a few more inches.... don't think of it!

I'm slowly cleaning the pins from a steep pitch at the top of the dihedral, but below me the rope jams again; I rappel down to free it and start back up on stirrups and jumar ascenders. Sudden rumble/explosion: the rope has dislodged a cluster of big flaky blocks, they cascade down on my head. By the time I can duck it's over, I'm only scratched—but no, don't move! There is one more block, a big one, teetering some fifteen feet above me, pinned, held in place by the rope I'm standing on. I hold my breath. If it falls and cuts the rope, well.... George is just above on a small snow-covered stance; he sees, understands, throws me the end of another rope. That way they can't both be cut if the rock comes down. I tie on, still holding my breath, then slowly shift my weight to the other stirrup. Ouf—the block tumbles, hits me in the face, falls into my arms. I manage to hold on to it, turn in my slings and heave it off, safely beyond our ropes. My gloves are red with blood, but it's only a cut lip. On we go....

Just below the summit, standing in a kind of notch out of the wind, that roars up the dihedral at gale force. We're soaked and shivering and we have to take our sweaters off to wring out the sleeves. We lower George into a gully, he disappears around the corner and ultimately, the hauling line leads up at a cockeyed angle over an immense overhang. I'm too tired and impatient to be careful and when I swing out on it, I find myself hanging five feet from the wall and screwed up higher than Hogan's goat:

I've rigged everything wrong, my slings are so short I can't move, my safety loops are somehow clipped into each other and not the rope.... It takes a while to get everything straightened out but I do, and now, moving slowly up this yellow-green thread into the sky I get another nasty surprise. The rope is icing up, and time and again my jumar clamps suddenly come loose, dropping me with a thump, so that only the extra Gibbs ascender clipped on top of everything, just in case, keeps me from dropping to the end of the rope every few feet. It's too much, I'm really getting psyched out and call up for a top rope just in case. Once more George saves the day, although it's probably all psychological.

Chris has been waiting in the wind through all this, and now he's too cold to lead on, so George takes the last pitch, disappears over the black, hoar-frosted summit ridge. We're up. I'm the last one off the face. The rope is an icy white cable. As I clean the pitch there is a momentary clearing, the mist parts below me. A surreal vision: snow-plastered slabs dropping into the Witches' Cauldron, the giant twin Cats Ears spires rising out of the gloom under my feet, so cold, so hostile, so beautiful.

The clouds close back in: On the other side of the summit ridge, George and Chris are shoveling out a bivouac ledge like demons, clouds of spindrift pour over them, a snowslope shelves steeply off into the greyness. The summit is up there in the mist but it looks easy, we're here, we're up, and tomorrow....

    No summit
          no mountain
      no earth

> only
> three shadows
> walking
> on top of
> mother of pearl clouds
> no climbers
> no climb
> no victory
> no defeat

Afterwards came another wet cold bivouac, another day, another bivouac, another day. Our fiberfilled sleeping bags, soaked and frozen, somehow keeping us warm and alive. Our soggy feet and hands carrying us, lowering us, carrying us again, over the top and down, and down, and down.

A few moments snatched out of the mist: the top or thereabouts (a series of bumps on a long thin ridge, who knows which?) where we spent an hour or two moving above the clouds. Our shadows accompanied us on the clouds some few hundred feet below, each inside its own rainbow halo, Brocken spectres.

There was our happiness at finding two of Fred Becky's old rappel rings from his first ascent of the mountain in forty-eight. Just to think that somebody else. And then at last the glacier, an out-of-focus world of subtle shades of grey:

> Cloudwalkers,
> or fallen angels,
> we stumble forward
> across the
> uncertain interface
> of snow and sky.
> Why escape?

> We may already
> have left the earth
> far below us
> to keep company
> with invisible gods,
> tramping silent circles
> thru the infinite
> white on white
> of endless clouds.

It was whiteout city, but we just kept on trucking. And sure enough there was an end to it. The edge of the high Stikine plateau, the escape route into and through the icefall; and four-thousand feet lower down, after we'd run like madmen under the last ice cliff, jumped the last crevasse, our beautiful blue tent was still waiting for us.

After six long days, we took off our rope, threw off our packs on the moraine, kicked off our wet boots and smiled at each other and the world. This time the crooked road had led us straight. We'd been to the far North and back.... The journey was over and no longer mattered.

That too was OK, and still is.

> Thank you lord for rest days:
> for sun on the boulders,
> for camp in disorder
> with drying ropes and
> clothes and bags and all
> our rainbow colored junk
> spread out around us.
>
> Thank you for this lonely place
> for these empty miles
> of cracked glacier tongues,

for these stark grey walls
towering into the clouds;
for letting us be here
where we don't belong.

Thank you for these safe sounds:
the rain on our tent fly,
and not on our faces
under soaked bivy sheets,
the roar of ice cliffs
collapsing high above
and far away.

Thank you for our mountain
which frightened us
but didn't kill us,
for a safe route down,
a world to return to,
friends and women to love,
for today and tomorrow.

The Cado

The Fourth of July
on the East Face of Mt. Morrison

A SMALL AND PATRIOTIC VOICE tells me that it's today, the Fourth of July, neither yesterday nor tomorrow, since yesterday was nothing but a midnight drive through Carson City desert flats, past shuttered Basque cafes, down sleeping 395, through eyeless Bridgeport ribbon asphalt, sleeping in the car while Cado drives; and tomorrow
                                                        will only be Cado waking me up on our narrow bivouac ledge 800 feet above the snow at first pink in an eastern sky, last sip of tea, finish the lead in the cold, moving stiffly, free the jammed red rope and on, up steep crumbling limestone to find a small stance, put in four lousy anchor pins that can't possibly hold, the Cado weighs so much more than I do, climbs up to me in the dawn and on past, hoping he doesn't; won't; can't slip, but of course he can't since today is truly the fourth and already skyrockets are banging and farting their colored stars across the Sierra sky while star-spangled banners unfurl in the wind from broken summit towers to the frantic cheers of the crowd below, empty boulder fields and scrub trees beneath high snow, dropping down toward the lake, our shoulders all sore and raw from the long approach, heavy packs up an endless hanging valley,

     hanging now in stirrups above the Cado who belays from a flake in the middle of this overhanging headwall, guillotine flakes badly balanced, ready to crash in a thousand pieces on the white-bull's eye of the Cado's hard-hat thumbtacked onto the exact center of this dizzy triangle view: glacial wings stick out on either side of the plunging buttress, cosmic moustaches, mountain sunlight trapped and echoing inside my dark glasses, rotten holds above me, all backlit, sparkling and fuzzy as I look up, move up, finally pull up onto a sloping ledge with no place to belay, no piton cracks, no solid blocks, no nothing, have to go further, traverse left with the sideways sun, frightened of the crumbling rock, jammed between wobbling blocks, but Cado at least is safe now below the overhang, and the fourth now is nearly over,

                                        night falls out of nowhere on the promised ledge, our feet dangle above a slow bay sunset while the first rockets explode high over Sausalito and the dark water stretches east like a desert night, fitful dreams of a cramped bivouac flame out across the Sierra sky with shooting stars, halfway from sudden night to tired dawn, wrapped in downies and cagoules, held in place by nylon hands, and my gal too is there in the milk of a two-thirds moon, after the shouting and the fireworks have died away, the red and green riding lights of the boats drifted off toward Nevada, standing on a shattered ledge just out of reach, wrapped round and round in the stars-and-stripes of a dream bivouac, her breasts two marble hand holds above a torn old flag, crumpled moonscape, spilled ink, black puddles on black lakes,

    moon shadow of the north ridge all jagged across the snowy valley, splintered jawbone of a shadow-mountain beast, all these different pictures dancing on my narrow ledge, wide-angle and close-up, perfectly exposed on midnight emulsions, that I discover each time I wake, halfhanging against my anchor, greys, heavy black brush strokes, shivers, and Cado slumped beside me, feet in slings to keep him on the ledge, hibernating bear in moonlight, check my anchor, carabiners, knots, look for water, none, see her again through half-closed eyes, far enough away I can't hear what she's saying as she spins slowly away in her red-white-and-blue moon rags, the last holiday sparklers still burning in her underwater eyes,

            and I can only try once more to edit this last scene into something coherent, but all this transparent film is strung in tangles down shadow cliffs, I can't find the shots I need, waking-shifting-dreaming-sleeping dissolve into each other without pause, the sharp stone digging into my back alone is real in this fantasy of a Sierra night after so many weeks in the city, and tomorrow, the other, the real tomorrow is no more real than these fourth-of-July fragments superimposed in a dishonest montage across the magic ektachrome of my mind.

in Mountain Gazette, year one, July 1973

Looking up at the Grand & Mt Owen

With Daredevil on the Grand Traverse

I

TETON EVENING INFINITIES. A pipe beside us on the wooden table. Haze and dust from the corrals condensing into dusk. Thickening anodized aluminum light in the darkness of our wine. Forest sounds: slurp of spaghetti against the cricket evening, pine needle pad of feet, music and words mixing with packhorse smells against black pine....

> *Jewels and binoculars hang from the head of the mule*
> *but these visions of Joanna*
> *make it all seem so cruel*

Slow words spiraling upward. Upwardspiraling wordchains from a plastic portable phonograph balanced in treetrunk shadow beside this table where we sit to dinner with friends. Last supper before a long climb. Our packs, blue and grey, packed and waiting on a fallen log behind us. Shadow summits waiting overhead. Patient slowed-down sunset giving us time to find our way out of this spiral maze of words, hanging heavy on grass-soaked air.

Behind us Canada. Summer snowstorms. Discouragement of undone climbs, false starts, long retreats. Endless miles across dusty summer wheat. Garage mechanics' greasy hands. Our car blowing up at last. Final oil-spewing gasps of a dead Volkswagen one Montana afternoon. Bright Montana sun beating down while Jim buys a used Ford sedan to take us on through the midwest night. Back to Wyoming and the Tetons. Himself afterwards home to the East. The sea and the city....

Still sitting here over a last glass of wine, while patient fingers fill a last pipe.... looking a last goodbye at those beautiful breasts under pearl buttons of a cowboy shirt. She hands me the pipe. Long shadows stretch and groan with added weight of darkness. Added last lungfull of smoke brings time to a reluctant halt. Record spins on in a pool of dark sound. The Stones take advantage of this lull in time to overwhelm the miniature amplifier. Jagger sings: I'm going home.... The Stones play on and on. Someone's cigarette hangs orange in purple air. I'm going home. And where is home? Up there, where black Teewinot squats like a dreaming toad above climbers' camp? Those other peaks beyond? Long days of sunlight and rock? We wait until we can move again. At last the music ends and for a moment we're free. We grab our packs and run.

Up sagebrush slopes toward the first canyon. Walking, trudging. Dreams of floating upward through seagreens and blues of evening underbrush. Slowmotion choreography. Reaching out to touch spiky leaves. Breathing damp sage. Shaking our heads in disbelief.... Canyon steepens, narrows. Swimming slowly with careful strokes not to disturb evening's submarine balance. Losing footing among moving shadows. We reach the first pines and there is no more light, fumble among trees for a first bivouac site, take off heavy packs, arrange pineneedle beds. We wonder at the scattered lights below and put on down jackets. Incomprehensibly we continue dreaming even after we fall asleep....

2

The scene fills slowly with an enormous boulder, foreshortened. Its form an irregular semi-oval, only a couple of sharp corners and, most conspicuously, a recessed almost-square plaque of lighter grey stone, as though a piece of the boulder some two-feet square had fallen out, or been knocked out of place, a visible scar against so much dark rock. We see the boulder from below so that more than half its surface is in the shadow, only the upper edge shining halo-like where sunlight bounces off a row of white quartz crystals, and the sides, where the boulder is wedged up against the walls of the chimney, appear only as darker shadows. Indeed it must have been ages ago, during its deafening, shattering fall between the steep walls of this chimney, that the square block of projecting stone was knocked off the otherwise regular surface of the boulder, at any rate, before it came to rest, jammed thirty feet above the bottom of the chimney, forming an overhanging chockstone that blocks its tenfoot width from side to side. The small white shape, however, wedged between the boulder and the right-hand wall can hardly date from that distant and cataclysmic fall, but instead comes into focus as a hand—the hand, or fist, of a climber who now appears spread-eagled on the wall of the chimney below. From his position, the walls must seem far smoother and more symmetrical than they really are, for instead of seeing the confusion or ledges and cracks that fragment these compact walls more and more as they widen and fold back into the face around them, he sees only two parallel planes, the left one already catching the morning sunlight, and both widening out into a haze of sunlit blocks above. This inaccessible sunlight does not, however, help him to pick out the details of his own right-hand wall, and we see him feeling blindly with his right hand for holds above his head.... Nor are the light and our own narrow perspective sufficient to indicate where this scene is taking place, where this chimney with its obstinate chockstone is located, on what mountain face. For that much is sure—the character of the rock, the view down past the sandy bottom of the chimney where the climber's companion stands, half in sunlight, squinting up at the other's progress, and taking in as well a vertical slice of the valley below, the rolling hills to the east—all this at least, tells us that the chimney is high up on the side of a mountain, and indeed an inspired guess might place it high on the East Face of Teewinot. But there or elsewhere, we simply have to admit that this scene, this vertical panorama of two climbers motionless between two rock walls, doesn't contain enough information to let us say anything else: to guess, for example, the outcome of the higher climber's search for a better hold, or even assuming that he finds one (since they are not roped up, perhaps it's not too difficult) and disappears upwards, followed quickly by his companion onto the easy summit rocks... and even if we could see, could guess all this, how could we construct the hypothetical continuation of their morning's climb, whether or not they continue down the other side: follow the confused ups and downs of the ridge, over the East Prong and on towards Mount Owen in the distance. How could we guess the heat and thirsty the search for melting snow, the hasty rappels, the sparkling slabs, the lassitude of a long ridge?...

3

Shattered doubtless by the Hammer of Mighty Thor, the ridge fell away in a succession of crumbling pillars, tilted pinnacles, broken walls—A Cosmic Slag Heap! And down through this maze our two Heroes threaded their Intrepid Way, employing now, for the first time, the full gamut of their Super Powers to vanquish the Gargantuan Obstacles that studded their way.

Daredevil is in the lead now, picking his way across a tiny ledge where, surely, human balance must fail and the hapless climber plunge toward the abyss! Apparently immersed in his own thoughts, his left foot is already poised above space, when...SWOOP!...

Warned at the Last Second by his highly developed middle ear, Daredevil barely managed to execute a Perfect Back Flip just as he started to fall, catching himself—Ahhh!... by one hand on the Brink of Eternity!

Instantly, his computerlike brain, which in everyday life allows him to masquerade as an ordinary New York trial lawyer, takes over! Realizing that this is more than even super balance can handle, he deftly fastens one end of his ultra-light line to the rock and hurls the rest into the yawning gulf below.... Keeping his cool, Daredevil signals with his free hand to his companion—Spider Man!

"Wow, Daredevil in trouble!" the younger of our two super heroes mumbles to himself as he moves out across the blank wall, exuding a special sticky spider substance from his feet and hands to accomplish the impossible.

"Hey! 'you sure this is the route?

—No doubt about it! replies Daredevil, hanging imperturbably from one hand on the brink of space, a feat for which long years' discipline in the mystic oriental martial arts had prepared him.

—Gee Daredevil, I mean, I thought I was used to steep walls, but this one, WOW!

—Here use my micro cord! I think your spider senses will come in handy.... down there!

—Some idea of yours, chum! this Grand Traverse! the spider youth mutters as he disappears from sight, rising to the challenge despite his tender years.

At last our Unstoppable Team stood reunited in the middle of a Sheer Face. The Perilous Descent of the South Ridge of Mount Owen was almost over, and soon they would be hurling themselves at the still more Horrendous Defenses of the Great North Ridge of the GRAND!.. Only time would tell if their Unique Combination of Super Powers was the key, whether they would emerge Alive and Victorious on the next and hardest summit.... when suddenly!...

THONK!... CRASH!... THUNK!...

"Holy Spider Gods! What was that?"

—Rockfall, old buddy, stay calm!

ZING!... ZWANG!... THUD!...

—I'm getting.... THONK!... out of here, Daredevil! Golly, aren't you afraid of anything?

—You're right. Spidey! Speed is of the essence.... CRASH!... Whew! That was too close for comfort, let's go!...

And on they went! Time and again they combined their Incredible Powers to vanquish Hideous Obstacles! What Curious Fate had brought these two legendary figures together to Accomplish the Unthinkable?

At the Notch: The North ridge looms above like a Suicidal Dare.... Off they rush to conquer the next obstacle on the GRAND TRAVERSE!...

4

Morning. High up on the West Face of the Grand. Moving stiff legs after a cold bivouac: gravel covered ledge where we emerged last night from the North Ridge. First dull red light through the nylon fabric of our bivy sack. Hissing flame of the Bluet stove warming a pot of tea.... Cold bleak scene: last few hundred feet of rock up to the summit of the Grand. Short steep walls and broken terraces. Late-summer tongues of water-ice hidden in grooves and gullies. Familiar granite texture, dull grey or pale tan in diffuse dawn light. Far below us the West Face shelving off into shadowy depths of still-sleeping canyons. A few more minutes, last sips of tea. Taking off our gloves and lacing our boots. Shivering a last minute on our ledge before starting for the top.

    The face above us seems quite complicated, but not hard enough to rope up. Several times we lose our way, back out of a smooth chimney to look for something easier. This narrow groove perhaps? A slanting ramp of ice running up its back? Jim has our only axe, goes first, cuts steps in the brittle surface. Hollow sounding blows and ice chips cascading down like dry leaves. Two steps, move up, two more steps.... But the walls narrow, converge on either side until finally Jim's pack jams as he steps up. Shit! A pause. Jim backs down a few steps, looks around, stuffs the axe into the straps of his pack, bridges out between the two walls.... Another pause. Looks around the corner.... Decision: Jim steps across the the right wall, balanced on tiptoes above my head, disappears around the corner!...

    I follow, use my hammer on the slippery ice, come to the bottleneck and move out on the rock, a foot on either side.... Look for holds to my right. Damn! but they look small! The rounded edge of the groove. Pale granite, almost pink. A few knobby crystals, not much!... Still Jim didn't have any trouble here; he would have said something; must be holds I can't see around the corner; only a few feet, come on, come on!... Long hesitation. Come on! okay! okay!...

A push.... now I'm across. Standing on the crystals with hands flat on the smooth rock. Very insecure. A few more moves. Next little bulge. Around the corner. *Oh la la!* This is nowhere. No holds in sight. I've been had.

Quick undisciplined thoughts bursting the seams of an inadequate moment, broken and laid open by my sudden, fear, enormous paralyzing fear. (I can almost see myself from above, from the next ledge, looking down to where I'm standing on the edge of a rounded slab, its steepness leads down and down, past the minor interruption of a small ledge, on down tumbled slabs into the morning depth of the West Face—the long trajectory of a tumbling bouncing fall that begins with any slip of insecure toes, that might begin.... Christ, what am I thinking of?... thinking of the red and yellow ropes inside our packs, wishing for an impossible belay, that bastard, that bastard McCarthy! how did he get across so easily? 'gonna get me killed, out of sight up there somewhere, can't even throw me a rope, certainly can't go back across, jesus! if I only had a few spider powers....) Hesitation. Unreal, too real fear. Falling. No handholds. Cold fingers. Those faraway breasts in a little tent. Hot springs, sunshine. Tall waving grass. So much fear. Thinking about thinking about being afraid. Stupid fear. Only twenty feet. Impossible.

And then it's gone, an unmeasurable second later. I start to move up: cautious, slow-motion, painful steps. Balancing on ridiculous crystals. A calmer fear still crowing like a rooster on my shoulder. But letting me breathe again, move again, swallow lungfulls of frozen blue air.... Climb the last few polished feet till fingers close around something sharp—I'm home!... That sonofabitch McCarthy! How did he do it so calmly? Daredevil! Those deceiving gold rimmed glasses! Ah well....

Hurrying on up easier terrain, catching up to Jim, scrambling to the summit, signing the register: "from Teewinot via Owen and the N. Ridge, en route to Nez Percé, 7:00 A.M." Another pause. Sunlight streams across the plains. Horizon haze and few wisps of cloud evaporating like used-up fear in layers of blue. (Well, luckily I did it....) All things in their place: even fear like a cold shower to begin a new day.

5

Heat...lassitude. 11:00 A.M. of an endless second day. Vertical sunlight. Slow...movement...upwards...slow. Endless talus. Broken boulders, above, below, underfoot, forever. Plodding...upward...hours. Heavy packs.

This mythic destroyed landscape, reserved by unloving gods to punish presumptuous men. Presumptuous or ignorant, but condemned to climb. Indifferently upwards.

Same foot lifted at each step onto the same grey flake. Same orange lichen on its edge. The slope itself moving and shifting. Higher blocks becoming lower blocks. No top nor bottom, up nor down to this endless slope.

Heavy packs. Heat...and...repetition. Thirst. Sun-struck talus slope leading to the top of South Teton.... Last snow bank. Long trudge. Careful footsteps on shifting blocks. Head bend down. Slow rhythm: step, up, step, up, step....

Looking up at paper cut-out rocks against a lizard sky. Last few ragged peaks standing in our way: the Ice Cream Cone, Mt. Spalding, Gilkey Tower, Cloudveil Dome. Ups and downs and detours of an endless ridge....

But first this damn slope! Must be covered with snow earlier on. Last few hundred feet. Heat...and...lassitude. Glaring light. Plodding... slowly...upwards.

6

Afternoon light. Evening satisfactions. Long ridge behind us now and the summit rocks of Nez Percé are turning color beneath our hands: tan to pink, white crystal veins, burnt umber, dull orange....

"Well, we did it, Spidey!" Jim looks for the register. Broken pencil stub, wrinkled paper: "First traverse, N to S, of the main chain, Teewinot to Nez Percé, Daredevil and Spider Man (J. McC. & L. T-F.), two days, perfect weather, Aug '66"

Such a small "first" after all. Summer's end. A modest "first" despite everything, to take back to camp, back to a wooden table and a gallon of wine with Teton friends and Teton faces in the dust of one more pause, tomorrow, before Jim goes east and I go west to separate cities on separate coasts. Another year around the corner. Yellow and red ropes in musty trunks. Cold mornings and all that fear. Drunken surreal landscapes, lost above clouds and in time.... All this, ready to be half forgotten, half remembered, never quite ending.

Late afternoon, for the first time threatening clouds are piling up to the west. Finding the right couloir down: narrow twisting gully, wet slabs, unstable blocks. Down and down. Opening out at last into a vast cirque of boulders, scree tongues, late summer snowbanks hidden in shadow above Garnett Canyon. First green trees far below....

Running! It's over! Running: mad flying steps down steep scree. Packs bouncing wildly on our backs. Sliding rock and gravel. It's over! Running, skating, leaping, sliding, falling, down long grey slopes.... It's over! Sliding, glissading, skidding sideways down dirty snow fingers. Laughing descent, lower, faster.... Finally now, bigger boulders, wildgrass and weeds, wet sand.... Standing out of breath beside the first stream.... Teton harmonies.... It's over!

Filming on Friz Roy

Fitz Roy, The Way It Wasn't

I

YOU NEVER CLIMB THE SAME MOUNTAIN TWICE, not even in memory. Memory rebuilds the mountain, changes the weather, retells the jokes, remakes all the moves. The Fitz Roy I remember isn't really the Fitz Roy we climbed—but it'll do. The longest approach in (our) history: leaving Ventura, California, in a used Ford van loaded with skis and surfboards. Four months later watching Yvon rebuild the engine on a sidewalk in downtown Santiago, Chile. Bluffing our way into Argentina with a two-dollar rubber stamp to modify the car's customs documents. Chris Jones, ace mathematician, figuring out that we'd need at least 200 pounds of sugar on the basis of one teaspoon per cup of tea, per meal, per man. Laughter all around. Buying a couple of pounds of sugar in Bariloche and heading south. Second ice-cave camp on the *Silla*, the seat, under the real rock, the real Fitz Roy, granite finger in the wind. Getting to know the wind, staggering around in the wind, wind-whipped snow looking great through the viewfinder of my Bolex wind-up 16mm camera. Hiding from the wind. Back up to the *Silla* with more food for more waiting, waiting for the wind to slack off, more wind, more waiting, ready to go, settling down to wait for that one clear day, more waiting. Almost there, we can almost taste it. Weeks of waiting, snug as a bug in an ice cave, telling boring stories, cooking boring food, writing a Funhog's gourmet guide to the world in Dorworth's tiny spiral notebook, complex rating systems, complex memories, simple conversations, always damp under the ice, weeks of getting nowhere, going nowhere, day after day, scraping snow off the entrance of our cave, seeing nothing....

2

The mountain out-waiting us. No more food. Back to base camp in a howler of a storm. Base-camp boredom just a variation on a bigger theme. Hiking back down to the road and driving out to buy more food at the nearest country store, more wine, cans of rancid butter from somewhere in eastern Europe. Chasing a lamb all afternoon with Tompkins, and then two amateur butchers butchering it. Back up into the forest, back into heavy waiting mode, composing crossword puzzles, devising fiendish traps to kill the mice that were eating the flour reserved for Yvon's bread. Morning body count: half a dozen dead mice floating in a cook pot of water after walking the plank and leaping for the suspended cheese, complicated Rube Goldberg traps that always got their mouse. Hikes to nowhere under stormy skies, rain in the forest, waiting becoming a lifestyle, time almost stopped. Nothing lasts forever but everything lasts for some time. A break in the weather says go, and we go. The weather says yes, and we say maybe, and keep going. After two months the lads so jazzed to be moving again that it doesn't matter if the damn Bolex is frozen, ticking over like a pocket watch in glue, just crank up the spring and hope for the best. The hidden geometry of our buttress fooling us over and over, ought to be there already, but a row of gendarmes says not yet. Looks like a bivy on the way down, no one gives a shit, after two months farting around under a high-speed sky worried about wind, we tell ourselves the weather will hold forever or at least till tomorrow. And then there's the slow evening trudge up the final bouldery, snowy slopes to the top of the Fitz. Everyone humoring me, the movie guy, but still hinting that I should hurry. We all hurry. Of course, we bivy on the way down. Dorworth and I will spend the winter teaching skiing at Squaw Valley, feeling our toes tingle from this night out in frozen wet boots.

Who cares? And then time speeds up: we're out of there, pooling our Argentine currency for a sea-food feast in the first restaurant we reach, flying home on New Year's Eve, crossing the midnight champagne line three times between Buenos Aires and California.

3

And now the story gets complicated, starts to blur, shifts to the screen of a little film-editing machine above the bay in Sausalito, where my buddies keep kicking the same steps up the wind-packed snow, back up, endlessly. Memory fights with reality and wins, climbing memories start to blend and lose themselves in film memories-to-be. Recording a wild sound narration track by loosening the lads up with lots of red wine while the tape recorder keeps running, collecting revisionist memories, stories of the climb replacing the actual climb, remembered conversations replacing real ones, half an hour of film chronology replacing our sixty days on Fitz Roy, ten minutes of good footage standing in for our eight clear days. Memory off on its own trip. The way it was, or wasn't. But what the hell, Chris Jones said it right there at the end of the film, not the wine, and I know it's true because I recorded it, I was there: "It was a good experience."

Fitz Roy

Fromage to Patagonia
.... or the sorry of Fats[1] Ray[2]

1 Domino
2 Charles

A chapter from the book *PATAGONIA: LAND OF PATAPHYSICIANS*
—*translated by Lito Tejada-Flores*

"Look," Oliveira said. "You know very well that I get dizzy from heights. The very name of Everest makes me feel as if someone had kicked me in the crotch. I hate a lot of people, but no one the way I do Tensing the Sherpa, believe me. "
—Hopscotch, Chapter 41, Julio Cortazar

Hew wood half gassed it wore so hardtooth clime, this cursent mounting? (Cryptich carving entree of ault Friends base-cramp—Illiad sink summons K. Newsome lay!)
Better go now, yah!
Spin rainsturming for weaks & leaks, & dozen up here lake it waste going to stoop in the immaculate few cheer. Patter go on yer tent roof, & this un-mens moundly, Fides Roi, lumping above with its presupposes all beadling down and glowered with eyes. Windblowy were the dice when frost we came to this inhospital blaze, & weary soon the whether braked our go hin.
With the straggle for camp won, weed highted many lows to the

happy of our snow grave or grotty (lots of womb as a mater of cornice!). But this was jest the be-grinning ...

Hard-headed for the cool war we sat out hoarly one more thing, to bash the rat up-fars to camp too. Yvon led hup the overfanging Berkshire (or "rimey" as the French poe it!) to a collar fulled with rotty sno. By laying from the rock we had fancied four why up the cool where to the call of the Italians, a breach of faith, to be slower; but it took two trays to clam the notch, where the wind hate us—wop!

Rock-haired wore the eyes benuff its sour face and all hour forts at craving were but fable. Foundly at fast, Chris fell in sight of a crevie which did us nasty for a nice cave. In two drays of hard weak we transmorted all the lows of food and care to our gravey, & at longing least were weedy for the flanel bush to the so-might....

A lace it wore not two be! The mourning found us agrain in a hoarful bliz-hard, sew fears the cold and batter the wind! While the blustard bloated & scrimed without the clave, we seated in for a long white. Hear betwo the gold eyes we lifed it up unter the slowstorm, fouling and scruming outsat the entrance. How to piss awry the time-off daze? becalmmed our problematic, & all through the prospectus for sunslight wah slow, we gamely classed a boot to divort or intertrain hour sleeves: many a stimulightening di-eclitic ensuited....

After a wild we lost truck of the pass sedge of time. Blurry I'd in the dim nest, & board stiff of tailing sorries. Naught to dew (re: en affaire, sat the Frogs)....

Too weaks thinner the whether hadn't all-turned & with no food laughed we head to re-tread. Hungry in deed down we want in a slate clearing. But even be low was no butter. Wood it hefer stop we wandered thru gloamy forest round windy crampfire? With erry break in the wurther we stormed back towards the craven hello of camp too. Some die we new a star-full sky must led us head for the top ...

Finely downed the somewhat day! We were aus at free of the clock, a cross the dark slowslope, stumping toward the call. We glommed the early patches in morning late. The ladders dropped ropes for the resting of us, and our jew mas brought us gentiley up. The cramping was fearly heart, yet airy-thing was going wall. Often on the blowing crowds hit the son but we crept on growing sledily.

Alta partically difficult sport we stopped foreign lunge, but the hoarfull chill bit us go on. Are boots wear wide with I's & no grueler scold was portable, had we been jason the colden freeze. A wild we weighted for Yvon the Torrebull to tickle a slimmery fifenine, but he jimmied up it known the least. Scrumtimes in a deep chilly the lead her really Doug in, splicing his beatons in fragile pot o'Ming crags. Soly, how effort, the obstacules were surmounded, & at long last we had a ridge view of the topo. Only a fued John-at-arms blacked our rut.

The aftersoon wore out as we clammed a-longing tortoise the top-mast summer. A last repeal sprung us to a notch belower its stop. We scrabbled uppers ful of eggspection overt bowl dirts & stowe. It restrained but to add the good ol' sum it! To gather we stomped fiveward onto the so might. The summa of the Fritz! To the arising scratched a see of clowns above a plain of ayes, allagory in evening sunlate ....

Could this really be the mist bootyfull somewhat we'd ever none?

Translator's note: The rest of the M.S. *appears mostly anticlimactic and, in large measure, incoherent; thus it seems best to end with a slow dissolve of the five companions standing above this majestic panorama, "over-grimed with un-motion .... "*

Part Three

Fiction

Cerro Torre

Rojo's Peón

ROJO'S *PEÓN* SITS GRAY AND SILENT on his big gray horse beneath a gray and angry sky. There is rain in the air, and wind, always wind, and the mended inspected fence stretches downhill from silent horse to silent cabin below, Rojo's *peón* looks at the mountains of cloud with tired wrinkled eyes; other mountains are hidden beneath these mountains of gray cloud. No one in these parts knows his real name, except perhaps Rojo or Rojo's father who hired him; not even Rojo's bookkeeper who pays him ten-thousand pesos every two months when he comes down to the *estancia* house to get provisions for his *puesto*. There was a time when Rojo's hands called him *"el Chilote,"* not because he came from the island of Chiloé, but as if to say "that no-good Chilean," but that was before he cut one of them across the face with his braided whip and rode away without a word, and that too has been forgotten. He is too old, Rojo's peón, for fighting or gossip or memories; he can still mend fences, ride his giant horse, keep the sheep from wandering too far up into the mountains. The years and the wind have abraded the rest. *Cosas patagónicas*, Patagonian things: time and bad weather, summer and winter, the little cabin unchanging, the wind that sweeps out of the mountains like the broom of God, *el viento blanco, el viento azul*, the white wind, the blue wind, this hard country south of the pampas at the edge of these hard terrible mountains. Up there now, those gringos from Buenos Aires....

Motionless on his statue horse, Rojo's *peón* lets his wrinkled gray eyes move across invisible mountains beneath swollen clouds: *el* Fitz, *la Torre*, the tower, and the big white one, and then the pass. It is insanity to go up there, so much ice, so much rock, When I was a boy we climbed, but the hills were brown and burning by the coast: we scrambled with the sun on our backs and the sea down below, blue like my horse's eyes, sparkling glass, the white walls and tin roofs of the port spread out, and our house, the third shack down in the little *callejón* fronted with plywood packing crates from Japan, our plaster virgin by the door with her flowers, little white flowers in a blue can of Esso marine-weight oil. Where did I find those flowers on such scorched brown hills? *Devociones de mi juventud*, boyhood devotions, and now I only live on horseback, and it's starting to rain. Too many, too much, these angry clouds.... And where is Chile today? On the other side of the mountains, across the ice and the sea too, I think. Lost like an old man. an old man on his horse watching the storm get worse, a daily occurrence here where there are so many storms, *cosas patagónicas*.

But why did the old man refuse to lead our horses up here to base camp? Surely he must have known where to find the path, the *sendero*, and it took us a day of searching in the rain. They say he's worked for Rojo for thirty or forty years, or his father. Rojo's father that is. Rojo's *peón*, that stupid old man just sitting on his horse like he was deaf and dumb, and Nestor talking to him so slowly, not at all like he does back home in BA, or anywhere.... And now he's been up there for a week, Nestor and that German, and it's storming so hard. I'm trying so hard not to worry. The wind snaps another dead branch off another tree. It falls on the wet ground beside the two orange tents.

The little camp at the upper edge of the forest, five or six miles from the grassy hill where Rojo's peón sits on his horse in the rain. The little camp right up under the *cordillera*, just below the moraine of the glacier that snakes up towards the high rocky peaks, the *cerro* such-and-such, *el monte* something-or-other, and behind above them all, the tower, *la*

Torre. Why did we ever come? We were so comfortable in Buenos Aires, so happy. She is crying in the little shelter of fallen logs covered with plastic tarps. The fire has gone out again and Julia doesn't care. She's been trying to keep the fire going for two days now, as the storm gets slowly worse and worse. But Julia is only a city girl, a Spanish lit major from Vassar, here to study the gauchesque novelists, Justino Zavala Muñiz, Benito Lynch. But spending a year in South America is one thing, coming up here to this horrible place is another. And the wedding next month? My parents are flying down on the fifteenth and Nestor said.... and afterwards he promised we'd spend a month on his family's ranch in Misiones. There aren't any mountains there, are there?... But Nestor is so rich, why does he have to do these.... More tears, more wind shaking the trees overhead, more rain.

The pile of wood that she dragged up so painfully is completely soaked now. The whole forest is a monochrome blue. In the clearing, where only a week ago they could see *la Torre* and all its satellite spires, there is only the belly of a great gray cloud hugging the earth. Yes, almost a week now. And Nestor spent that whole first afternoon chasing a lamb that had wandered this far up the canyon. I wouldn't look when he killed it, but I did help him barbecue it, a regular *asado* just like some band of old-time gauchos, but what would they be doing up here? They'd have more sense. I bet that old man hasn't come up this far in thirty years.... I'd rather have my nature in smaller doses. Sunday afternoon in Palermo, with all the flowers and Nestor being really adorable, like he can be sometimes, telling me how much prettier I was than all those Argentinian girls all around, all those couples so happy in the sunshine, so safe, and afterwards driving back into the city for supper in one of those open-air steak houses, all in a row down by the river.... What a spring, and in such a city, how could I have resisted? And Nestor's so perfect really; it's almost a cliché being so tall and dark, so charming. And I was so flabbergasted when he actually proposed and now, but oh, oh Jesus but I hope he's okay. This awful storm, this....

Awful storm indeed, like all Patagonian storms, becoming indeed more awful the farther one gets from the plains, from Rojo's peón on his sad still horse in a thickening drizzle; up through the beech forest and past the two trembling tents and the weeping blonde girl, where the rain comes tearing in windy sheets through the sad blue trees; up onto the glacier where a million snowflakes are trying so hard to fall, only to be scooped up by the wind and tossed another thousand feet in the air to try again. A full-blown Patagonian storm riding out of the wet emptiness of the *hielo continental*, the continental icecap, on the back of an antarctic wind, one of the thousands of Patagonian things, *cosas patagónicas*, which either turn men into philosophers or kill them.

The wind more than anything else is Patagonia. The wind that becomes visible as it hurls torn shreds of cloud in all directions at once, twisting, turning, doubling back, then roaring straight on in from the west with its freight of snow and frost. West wind, northwest wind, southwest wind, the devil's own wests. The wind owns everything here, this range of peaks, *la Torre*. We were crazy to think it could have been ours, even for a day, and we needed at least a week of good weather. A crazy gust of laughter shakes his cold body and passes on the wind. He hangs onto his rope that in turn hangs down out of the clouds and the swirling snow, leans forward and rests his forehead against the hoarfrosted rock. Half the time he climbs with his eyes shut, his goggles have been torn off somewhere, this morning? yesterday? Now he opens his eyes and sees nothing but moving whiteness, He leans on the rope, rubs his hands in the wet gloves, calls up! All right, Hansl, I'm down, *du kanst hinunter kom*—What's the matter with me? Why do I keep calling to him? Of course Hansl can't hearr me, Hansli's dead. Why do I keep forgetting he's dead? I must be in worse shape than I thought. Those two pitons just ripped away, like they were nothing, and he just stood there, half-covered by the avalanche, slowly sliding down the wall, scraping away the snow as he went; the bastard didn't say a thing, just looked up.... And he had half our pegs and all the extra rope, the bastard! and

I'm supposed to get down all this by myself, another thousand meters. ha.... but Nestor is too cold to laugh, and laughter becomes a hysterical trembling that shakes his body on its small holds. He has to grip the rope even tighter in a moving white vertigo. Little avalanches cover him. His red cagoule, like a priest's robe, is torn, wet, and frozen.

Nestor is so cold, so exhausted now, that there are many things he no longer understands. He is a middle term in a series of events that seem to him to stretch out far beyond this storm, beyond *la Torre*, beyond.... but the directions, the beginnings and ends, escape him, are only confused by so much snow. The letter from Munich three months ago filled with Hansl's naive enthusiasms: the two of us, you who know those mountains so well, rush tactics, overwhelm it, one big push, how can we lose? How can we lose? That's what she always said to any objections. Her stuffy New England family? Well they came around, didn't they? Children? How can we lose, you so dark and me so blonde? This goddamn snow! I can't see if I'm anywhere near the col. Snowing too in Bariloche when I met her: the little tea-room on the Avenida Mitre, right around the corner from the Vizcacha steakhouse, all the ski instructors down from *la Catedral* laughing in the corner in their blue parkas: Jorge, Diki, the Petrovic brothers, so warm in here the windows are all steamed up, can't even see the snow outside and there's Julia, all lonesome-blonde in the corner. The old German waiter will be back in a minute with his silver tray all full of pitons and slings so I can go on down, go home now, it's so late.

So long, so late, and they said they'd be back Thursday, two days ago, but Nestor's so strong he must be okay. Everyone knows he's the best climber in BA; they're jealous of him with all his friends at the television. I remember those stories in Bariloche even before I met him: so arrogant, you'll see.... And then in that tea-room after skiing, he just walked right up to my table, of course I was almost the only girl in the place, but so charming, really, and those drunk ski instructors making their slangy cracks that I couldn't understand, thank goodness.... I can't understand it, why does he want to climb these awful mountains, *la Torre* especially?

Those days of good weather, when we could see it looming up there at the head of the valley like a great big—no, I can't say it, my up-tight petit-bourgeois upbringing I guess.... Oh my God, what am I talking about? to whom? And look at everything, all soaked down here and now it's starting to snow. Oh dear, that means it's getting worse, and the fire's still out. What if they should come back right now, I'd better, oh, why, why would anyone want to do such a crazy damn-fool thing? No one can climb these mountains. No one will ever climb *la Torre*.

No, no, he shakes his head and turns his horse in the rain. Rojo's *peón* knows that no one will ever climb *la Torre*. People were not meant to climb these terrible mountains, nor these mountains meant to be climbed by *los hombres*. *Poco a poco se gana el cielo*, little by little one gets to heaven, but not by climbing mountains, not this sky, this heaven, there are too many clouds, there is the white wind. Up there it's always winter, and hard and terrible. Even this storm has grown worse as he watched: the wall of clouds blacker, more twisted by the wind. It has all happened before: year in, year out, deep snow in June and July, by November the thorny *calafate* turns green for horses and sheep to graze on, but even when the sky is blue the wind howls down out of the canyons, there is no peace in this land, these are not mountains for men to climb. And last year, those little men who came from Japan they said: they stayed three months at the foot of the mountains and went away with sad faces. We are going home. Enough of this foolishness, watching invisible mountains. *¿Tu entiendes, caballo mio?* You hear me, oh my horse? Rojo's *peón* is stubbornly proud of having resisted the *voseo*, the funny grammar of the pampas; he still says *tú*. But it has been easy enough, he has hardly talked to a soul these last twenty years. Long ago he wanted to remain a Chilean, not to accept their ways. But it no longer matters. He even drinks *mate* now; they give it to him in two-kilo paper sacks at the *estancia*. In his cabin the black kettle is waiting on a black stove. A man must drink something hot. *Vamos*, let's go, let's go down.

But that *mate* is so awful; it's the worst thing here in Argentina. Thank heavens Nestor drinks it with sugar, and Hans, of course, he can't stand it, like me. I'll just make some old-fashioned Liptons if I can only get the fire started. Why is everything so hard? And my hands are ruined, look: all scratched and black-and-blue.... Soaked worn abraded fingers, so many hours, days in wet gloves: sore, then numb and frozen, painfully thawed to be soaked again. So cold, so hurt, my poor hands. It's getting so I can hardly hang onto this rope. That's it, just keep banging them against the rock, one at a time, till the feeling comes back. Then I can pull this damn thing down and make another rappel, another! Christ, how many more to the col? and our fixed ropes. if they're still there.... And then a few more hours down to the glacier, easy going back to camp: the tents like giant orange butterflies in the dark blue-green forest, no more wind. Julia running out crying, a fire, tea. Julia taking off my boots and thawing out my feet.... It's so warm here. Why doesn't Hansl hurry? It's direct: the rope drops right down to the tent, right out of the clouds. He should have an easy time; once you're dead, you see, you don't weigh anything, just floating down.... Julia, don't cry so much! Julia, I thought about you up there, at night in our bivouac caves, coming down, even on that broken ledge where the rope got stuck.... Julia, we'll make love later on, I'm so tired, too tired, and I can't feel anything in my feet, my hands, Julia....

But Julia is in the tent, lying on her sleeping bag. crying quietly to herself. The fire is burning again, but already starting to sputter; an unwatched pot of tea is boiling slowly away, turning black in the smoke. Rain and snow are falling together; everything is wet.... Late-afternoon clouds arc already congealing into darkness: nothing has changed. How many hours of light? even here, so far south.... And if Nestor isn't back, doesn't come back this afternoon, then what? and why do I only think of Nestor, not poor Hans? and why poor Hans? And oh God, what's going to happen to me up here? Of course I know the trail down. But tomorrow, if he doesn't get back tomorrow, or the next day.... and I haven't even told him about the baby, of course, I wanted to wait till after.... But I promised myself not to think about Nestor getting hurt, dying, oh.... Her blonde hair, half-wet, half-tangled on the damp blue nylon of her bag, buried broken beautiful face, weeping muffled but steady; the rain muffled but steady, dripping down a thousand tree trunks; the wind muffled but steady. Another branch snaps, falls.

Up in the clouds, the memory of sharp needle-like peaks hangs like a bad dream. Or a good dream, but anyway just a dream twisted by the wind. Another small avalanche covers Nestor where he stands on the broken ledge. The cold snow on his face wakes him up. Once more he starts to kick his boots against the rock, bang his hands, one at a time, against the snow-covered rock. Nestor looks up. The rope is still hanging down, still stuck; somewhere up there in the clouds the little knot has jammed at the edge of an overhang, in a crack. Jesus how can I tell? *¡Hijo de la gran....* son of the great whore who bore it! Nestor rocks back and forth, dizzy, cursing without conviction. Things are beginning to repeat themselves. How many times already has he tried to pull down the rope? As soon as the feeling returns to his hands he can try again. Hurry! It looks late already and Hansli had the bivouac sack in his pack when he fell. No shelter tonight. And no room to sit down on this stupid ledge. But if I can't pull this goddamn rope down it doesn't matter, it doesn't matter if I can live through another night, doesn't matter if I fall asleep again....

Sleep: I must've dreamt of Julia. Well I can always dream. but it isn't just a dream. I know there must be a fire down there, tea boiling in a little black pot. Julia must be awfully worried, poor girl. I should have left her in BA. Even life in camp is too tough for her; the tents look like giant orange butterflies coming closer through the trees.... No, no, I won't let it happen again. My hands are starting to hurt, a good sign. In a minute I'll try again. *¡Hijo de la gran puta que lo parió!* Two days ago the two of them had been so close to the top, the great ice mushrooms, of the summit and then..... But no, Nestor himself is no longer sure if they made it or not. When did this storm start? when will it end? In a minute I'll be there. Julia's waiting in her sleeping bag, warm and naked. I'm almost home.

Rojo's *peón* is almost home. His horse ambles down a little wash and up the other side. It's raining lightly and there's his cabin, his *puesto*. Rojo's *peón* has been thinking of the *gringos* from Buenos Aires, up there on *la Torre*. No, they are only men, as I too am a man. They are not able to do such things. No one can climb *la Torre*. And that pretty blond, *la rubia*, what can she be doing up there? what crazy dreams drove them to come here? to go up into those clouds?... I too, but my dreams are only of the sea. My dreams are full of sunshine, the dreams of an old man, dreams of my youth, just dreams.... There is so much one cannot explain. Patagonian things. *Cosas patagónicas.*

Ascent magazine 1971

....*up here is lonesome and cold*....

Who Goes Up Must Come Down

THIS IS THE STORY OF A MAN who climbed too far, and too high, who climbed past himself. It is impossible to know if this is the end of the story, or the beginning, or the middle. The man, the climber himself, doesn't know. He seems dazed, as though he's trying to wake up from a stubborn dream, from a hangover.

—*I'm going to die up here.*

Up here is lonesome and cold, and very very high. The top of a peak, a big one, a giant, and until a few moments ago, until the man reached its summit, the highest unclimbed peak in the Himalaya, that is to say, in the world, Gyangtse II.

—*I'm going to die up here. This time I've done it, really done it, pushed it too far, my luck and my limits. I've gone over the line. I'm going to die up here.*

Just thoughts, not words, not sounds, the man, the climber, is sitting in the snow, on the very top of this giant of snow and rock and ice. Not really sitting, sprawled out, motionless, his lips don't move, nothing moves.

I

The same thought over and over: *This time I'm going to die up here.*

Slowly, awkwardly, the way a retarded child assembles painful sentences, he thought:

Because now there's no way. No way. No way I can climb back down this ridge. No way. But I did it. I climbed the mother. The big one, Gyangtse II—a first ascent, by a damn hard route.... solo too.

A perfectly successful Himalayan expedition except for one thing: *I'm going to die up here.*

But thinking was too damn hard. Just breathing was hard enough, not breathing really, only gasping, gasping for air. The man lay gasping on his back on top of a mountain in the middle of the sky.

The mountain, Gyangtse II, a border peak, immense sentinel summit between Nepal and China, a giant pyramid of rock and ice, poking up through the clouds to over 26,000 feet, just a few feet shy of 8,000 meters, almost to the sky, almost to heaven. And on its very top now, motionless in the snow, this man, smaller than an ant.

Already late afternoon. Somehow, the weather was still holding in one last, pre-monsoon lull. Thick clouds boiling in the deep valleys beneath the peak. But up here, the high-altitude sky was still a deep, inky, blue-black. A sky empty of clouds, empty of oxygen—air too thin, too cold, too hard to breathe. And intruding into this lifeless sky, the mountain seemed, as always, too white, too pointed, too perfect. On such a scale the man hardly existed: a speck of dust pinned by the full weight of heaven against an indifferent anvil of ice.

The climber sprawled in a small depression in the snow, a couple of feet below the actual summit of Gyangtse II. Motionless, propped against his pack, gulping air. He shaped another thought:

I don't belong here, no one does.

And then concentrated again on breathing, took ten, fifteen, twenty more inadequate, un-oxygenated breaths, survived a fit of dry coughing, then out of nowhere, remembered a line he had memorized in the public library in Pasadena, a pseudo-Spanish Southern-California, tile-roofed sanctuary flanked by palm trees where he used to search for books on Mt. Everest, years before his first rock climb, just a kid mad about mountaineering, about the idea of mountaineering, a particular, peculiar and personal idea of mountaineering that he had made for himself in a southern California where the only mountains, the San Gabriels, rising above Los Angeles were always hidden in thick smog. He remembered that beautiful, rumbling, romantic, and provocative string of words:

...*the high Himalaya, highest peaks on earth, rooftop of Asia and the world, dwelling place of demons, gods, and storms, a kingdom of ice and wind.*

True. True enough. A kingdom of ice and wind. Now only the wind shared this summit with him. It came roaring, then screaming, then whispering over him, around him, through him. The wind was blowing a long scarf of ice crystals hundreds of yards out to the west—a streamer, a ragged white prayer flag of ice flying from the very top of the peak. Only the wind moved. Nothing else was moving, nothing else mattered.

Stacking words together in slow motion—awkwardly, painfully— he thought:

Doesn't matter.... does it? Don't know. Don't know if it matters. If I get down from here or not? Obviously I can't, so it can't matter—right? Right? Getting up mattered! Mattered enough to do it. Mattered enough to burn my bridges, cut off my retreat, overcommit myself. Jeezus! What an understatement. The last possible day. Our last chance to go for the summit, and I took it. Had to—right? Right? No one else was ready. Couldn't hesitate. Should have hesitated. Didn't. But it mattered, bet your ass it mattered. And it worked. I made it. A solo ... first ... ascent ... a big one ... the biggest one left in the Himalayas.

—That's what you always wanted, isn't it? What you've been dreaming about, ever since you were a teenager?

—Well no, not quite. No, not like this. Not with Hank and Peter swept away by that fucking avalanche. Not exactly the kind of solo first ascent I had in mind. No, not ending like this. Done in, fini, fucked up, kaput, ready to die on top of this damn mountain.

—Ready to die? Really? Ready? You're really just going to die here, without a fight? Don't you care?

—Should care, but I don't. I got here, I climbed the mother, and I can't even remember why. But I did it, that's all that matters. And Christ, look at me now.

A toy soldier with broken matchstick legs. A Michelin-tire man in tubular down clothing, deflated in the snow. Beaten, broken by the wind, but more by the altitude, by the lack of air, by the long brutal climb up the southwest ridge to the very top, to this symbolic nowhere, to this end, to this dead end.

The climber was a young man with an old man's face. His skin cracked and peeling—a scruffy black beard, dozens of dark crisscrossing wrinkles, open crevasses in prematurely aged skin smeared with zinc oxide, swollen lips, eyes hidden behind mirror lenses—empty sparkling reflections of an empty blue-black sky. On his face, instead of an expression, the climber wore an incomprehensible map of an unseen battle. A lost battle—won, then lost.

In all this space, inside the charmed circle of this hundred-mile horizon, among these surreal snow peaks marching south toward the Ganges plain, and north toward Lhasa, there was no one else, no one, no one else above this roof of clouds. Just one climber, on top of one mountain. Beside him an ice axe rammed into the snow. A broken scarecrow of a climber dressed like a clown, a puffy yellow down jacket, flapping red wind pants—colorful, frozen despair. Oblivious to the wind, tugging at him, tearing at him, packing crystals of spindrift around him, into every fold of his clothes, every exposed pore of his face. Staring blindly out over the great cloud bank to the west. Just breathing. Not thinking. Not moving. Just breathing, just trying to breathe.

Movement here is improbable at best. Life itself, at these altitudes, in this thin air, is highly improbable. Here few men could hope to breathe, to walk, much less to climb. Climbing in these Himalayas, these great border peaks separating India, Nepal, Pakistan, China and

Tibet, has always been reserved for a very few, for very strong, and very determined climbers. Tremendously fit, patiently acclimatized, obsessively motivated. Of these few, this dedicated half-mad handful of European, American and Japanese climbers who set out, year after year, season after season, for these enormous peaks, fewer still reach the actual summits. In the Himalaya mountaineers meet defeat more often than victory. They take greater risks, pay higher prices than they do at home. Those not destroyed by these mountains are always changed by them.

Trying to shape oxygen-starved ideas into patterns that almost made sense, he thought:

This doesn't make sense. I don't get it. Didn't know I was this far gone. Hell, I was in the best shape of anyone on the expedition, the best shape of my life, stronger than anyone else. But the expedition's over now, isn't it? Should have been stronger, though, much stronger. Those last towers on the ridge—so damn hard, so technical, 5.9, maybe 5.10, ice-covered rock, shallow, rotten, iced-up cracks.... badass stuff.... But I was climbing so well, really well.... And then the altitude finally hit me, right after the last tower, on that damn snow ridge, that last easy ridge to the top. Five breaths for each step, then ten, then I lost count. And all the time it was getting easier, the angle easing off. I knew I'd made it, only I was getting weaker step by step. I was crawling. Crawled to the goddamn top. As far as I could go.

—*So what's the matter now? Run out of strength? Or run out of ideas?*

—*It's not the same thing. Just ran out of energy, that's all. Just too damn high for that kind of climbing. No more energy. Like some spring inside me broke, snapped. No more strength, no more nothing. Almost 8,000 meters, die Totenzone, the death zone. Still I got here.... on all fours.*

—*So why don't you move? do something?*

—*Can't move. Maybe I could rest a little, take a little nap here, if it wasn't for this goddamn wind. At least I can still feel the wind. Aside from that I've gone numb. Frostbitten feet for sure, been that way for hours. But now my hands are going, even in down mitts. Maybe from sitting like this. Motionless. Got to move.... Can't move.*

—Pull yourself together, Miles, pull yourself together.
—Leave me alone for Chrissakes. What the fuck is this? I'm alone. I am alone up here, alone damnit, and now I'm hearing voices....

The climber twisted his head to look behind him. Nothing. No one. He coughed, pushed himself upright with both elbows, then both hands, clumsy in down mitts. Sat up and looked around. Shouted in a voice he couldn't recognize, out of a cracked, dried-out throat that was no longer his:

A solo ascent goddamnit. By. My. Self. And now I'm hearing voices. I'm alone, okay? so leave me the fuck alone!

No answer. Only the wind. Screaming, whispering, howling. Sitting up and yelling, the climber had forgotten to breathe, had stopped breathing. Too much effort, too little air. Half-consciousness dissolving seamlessly into unconsciousness. Blackness replacing whiteness, pitching forward in slow motion, face-first into the snow.

It was evening. It was always evening when he finally got to Nicole's place. Sunset colors—only smog could produce such stunning colors—slanting over the mansard roofs above the rue de la Victoire. Sidewalks jammed with bodies, all Paris giving up and going home. Nicole worked odd hours, always got off early, she would have been home for a couple of hours already. And she wouldn't be happy at the news.

'But you promised,' she'd say. He always promised. He never kept his promises.

'But you promised. *Tu as promis! Tu as promis!*' Yelling at him, hammering on him with two small fists. 'You promised. After Alaska, after that big first ascent and that big fall, no more expeditions, that's what you said. Are you crazy? Yes, I know you're crazy, you drive *me* crazy. You only think about those damn climbs. That's why you came back to Europe, back to Paris, back to me. You think I'll always be here, waiting....'

He watched her. Her eyes flashing and crying simultaneously. Those big grey eyes. Almost enough to make him change his mind, every time, but not quite. Give up these crazy big ideas of bigger crazier climbs, just enjoy rock climbing for fun, climbing on friendly crags, in the sun, above the blue Mediterranean water of les Calanques, with Nicole, the perfect climbing chick, his perfect French girlfriend, the perfect life, only it wasn't. He wanted to go, needed to go, and she would get over it, she always did.... so far. But this trip, this invitation to join the Alpine Club expedition to Gyangtse II, unexpected, out of the blue. But he deserved it. Damn it! Hell, who'd had a better season last year? No one. Miles was the top American big-mountain climber, big-wall climber too, almost. That two thousand foot face he'd soloed in Alaska last summer, that was the cherry on the cake. Should have sealed the deal, gotten him a place on any expedition heading for the big prizes. If he hadn't been such a hard-ass jerk. Truth was, no one wanted to climb with him anymore. That's what had pushed him into solo climbing—but a helluva way to make a reputation. And get killed, when things go wrong, with no backup. A little fall turning into a big fall, a zipper, pulling out all his aid pieces, all his pro, pins and nuts, one after another from those shallow cracks as he fell, and fell, and kept on falling. And finally stopped. Swinging in space, fifty feet out from the cliff face, spinning slowly in a bad dream that wasn't a dream. He'd passed out, blacked out, and woken up slowly, hurting. The rest too was slow and painful: climbing that perlon rope back up 50 meters to the one anchor pin that had held. Trying to rest in his slings, passing out again, bivouacking again, and somehow, the next day finding a new line of cracks, making a new start, pulling if off, finishing the climb. And he hadn't even dropped his camera. The photos showed he'd done it. Those jealous bastards in the Alpine Club couldn't say anything, didn't. And life went on. Back to the Alps for another season, back to Nicole, his perfect French climbing chick, too perfect for someone who only wanted to climb. And then the telegram, Gyangtse II? Can you join us? Hell yes. Nicole would get over it. She always did, didn't she?

2

The man, Miles, is no longer hearing voices—his voice? whose voice?—shaken awake now by a wave of dry coughing, half-strength coughing that hurts like hell, everything at such high altitude is half strength, everything hurts like hell. He rolls over, face down in the snow and starts to push himself upright again with awkward arms, flailing in slow motion, up, up, part way up, on hands and knees now, still coughing....

It hurts, at least I can feel it hurting, I'm still here, must have passed out, slept maybe, what a dumb idea —taking a nap on the goddamn summit. I like feeling this bad because at least I'm feeling something, but is that good? I'm still stuck, worse than stuck, I'm trapped. Trapped up here. This is some kind of stupid place to die....

On his knees now, looking around. Grabs his ice axe with two hands, supports himself on it.

Gotta breathe, can't breathe. Gotta get outa here, off this fucking mountain. Can't. The route's too damn hard to climb down. Guess I knew that, figured I'd find another route down. But where? What? What was I thinking? Couldn't ever see past that last ridge from Base Camp. Figured there'd be something. Is there?....

No.

Or is that?... Maybe? Can't tell. Can't really think straight, sure as hell can't breathe. Can't tell. But if I could get down a bit, say a thousand feet, maybe I could breathe easier, maybe think better. Maybe figure something out.... C'mon.

A big effort, pushing on his ice axe, off one knee, on his feet now, still looking around:

Chrissakes, over there, to the north, the Chinese side, sloping off, looks easy, not too steep, maybe a way off this damn peak, a way down.... Anyway, I'll feel better, c'mon, move.

And he moves.

Walking now, more like staggering at first than walking, across the small dimple of the summit. Miles moves, using his ice axe like a cane. Walking. Ever so slowly. Clumsy, yeah, but walking, walking. Not climbing, just walking. Down. No need to climb here. The snow is hard and wind-packed, a white path. He is not even breaking through, not sinking in. The north side of the summit, the north flank of the mountain, the Tibetan side, the Chinese side, starting out gentle. From here there's only one direction: down. *The snow in front of me. Down.* And this isn't just another narrow knife-edge ridge, but a kind of shoulder, big, rounded, white, sloping off toward the Tibetan plateau, somewhere down there, brown and barren, almost visible through a confusion of clouds.

Shaking his head, still working for every breath, every thought, still coughing from time to time but a little less now, Miles knows where he's going: *down. Just down.* That's all that counts. That's all that matters, he is starting to think it matters, maybe it matters. Keep walking. Don't trip. Swing each foot wide enough that the spikes of his crampons don't catch his wind pants.

The drug of movement, remembered movement, rediscovered movement, one step, then another, one step, then another. He likes the feeling, recognizes the feeling, like waking up, struggling back to consciousness after a drugged sleep, one step after another. Not strong steps, but still steps, real steps, and almost immediately, almost miraculously, after how many steps? he isn't counting, no need to count, but suddenly no more need to stop every few steps to breathe, to gasp, to wrestle more air, more oxygen into his lungs. *Because it's downhill,* he thinks. *I'm letting myself fall, step by step, instead of trying to lift myself like a dead weight....* It almost makes sense, but not quite.... *But I'm not really falling, am I? just walking, walking down a ridge....* A big shoulder turning slowly back into a ridge, narrowing, ever so slowly narrowing, every 50 meters or so, from a wide escape hatch, a highway, into—what? a trap? He can't tell, part of him doesn't care. He's moving and it feels good, not really good, but better. Just moving. Keep moving.... And he does, another 50 meters, then 100 more, *a rope length, another rope length*, he thinks, *although I'm not roped up to anyone now, but a rope length anyway, then another one, and another....*

He blinks. *Where the hell am I going?* The ridge is now a real ridge, no longer a wide and friendly snow shoulder. No longer an easy ridge, no longer a highway. Now it's bent, kinked and twisted. A tower of ice, squat but steep-sided, bars the way. Miles can see the ridge beyond it, curving down and back to the left into sight, still there, still friendly, still waiting for him. But he can't get there. *Damnitall!* he starts to shout, a hoarse shout that ends in a whisper. *Damnitall! knew it was too easy. It was. Too damn easy, and now it's too damn hard.*

A few more steps, right up to a kind of corner. Look around the corner: A drop off, steep, not vertical but steep, really steep, and blue, shining, glistening blue. Real ice not wind-packed snow. What now? Better sit down and think. Only thinking ain't easy. Sitting down is easy.

The germ of a decision: growing out of nowhere, growing inside him. Somewhere, something of that other Miles, the hot-shot ice climber from Colorado, is waking up. He knows how to cross this ice wall—he doesn't want to do it, Hell, he doesn't want to do anything, but here he is, moving, sort of. Getting some strength back, sort of, as he descends. Every 100 meters lower it's better. Miles grabs another deep breath and wrestles himself back to his feet, looks around the corner again: that same sheet of ribbed blue ice, arcing off sideways toward that distant shoulder that has to be the continuation of his same ridge, his friendly ridge. Maybe he can do it. The old familiar calculus. What if?

And if I can't, if I slip, if I'm just too weak to get across, well.... the ice wall stretches out across the mountain to safety, relative safety, and below him it drops away, drops down, almost out of sight, no, truly out of sight, toward a tangle of swirling clouds rising up from the Tibetan plateau. Steeper and steeper the lower it drops, disappearing way down there, "like the belly of a pregnant woman" his French climbing partner

used to say when the slopes beneath them steepened out of sight. *Either way, if I stay here I'll die, if I fall off I'll die. What the fuck.*
—*You can do it.*
—*What do you know?*
—*Don't forget your other ice tool, it's clipped to your waist.*
—*Jeezus, I can't even think straight. How am I going to do this?...*
Remembers his north-wall hammer, the mini hammer-axe at his waist, reaches for it. Checks his crampon straps. Tight. Slips his ice-axe sling over his wrist. Turns in, faces the slope. Shuffles a step or two left. The world tilts up in front of him. Snow becomes ice. Front points bite. *Here goes nothing, here goes everything....*

3

The slow-motion ice-dance. He had surrendered to it, not joyously, no adrenalin rush this time—did he have any more adrenalin left? Whatever happened to the adrenal glands at high altitudes anyway?—not with a rush but with resignation. He was no longer a climber but an ice crab, crabbing sideways across these fluted wind blasted ice cliffs toward the safe landing of that rounded snow shoulder 200 meters away.

Above a certain altitude there are no safe landings, he thought. But mostly he didn't think. Mostly he moved. That was progress. That was enough—just moving. Even in slow motion. The ice dance is always danced in slow motion but still, this was an extreme case: a frozen fumbling ballet of toe points hitting the ice, feet like lead, lifting, kicking, lifting, kicking again, finally sticking. The parrot's beaks of his two ice tools, his ice axe and his north-wall hammer, pecking into the brittle white crust. Arms like lead, lifting the tool, swinging it, the axe glancing off, lifting again, swinging again, finally sticking. One hand, then the other, one foot, then the other, slowly, in patient mechanical sequence, stepping sideways, tiptoeing sideways, crawling sideways across a 60 degree wall of ice, on all fours—four separate moves and his body would be one foot further left, one foot closer.

It was a long way to go—his mental numbness was an advantage, too drained to think beyond the next placement of the axe in his left hand, the next slow swing of his boot, crampon points crashing dully back into the ice.

That distant snow shoulder way over there was an out-of-focus blur on the far edge of his mind. A long way and a far cry from the real ice ballet he'd always loved so much on the frozen waterfalls of Colorado: swinging, swarming up those glistening translucent columns of water ice, giant icicles 20 or 30 feet across, a rainbow oil slick of reflections leading up into the blue Colorado sky. Now the sky was black, now he was moving sideways in order, perhaps, to go down. Perhaps. Perhaps not.

To go down. No, that was too far in the future. This was simply ice purgatory. He was dancing sideways until the music stopped. If he fucked up here, that would be that. The 32-feet-per-second-per-second toboggan down into China. Return to go. But don't start again. Never start again. The end. Somewhere inside he found the spare energy to smile, once. That was enough. Refocus the mind, the hand, the right hand. Swing the axe. Swing it right. This time the pick bites and holds.

Christ, no place to rest out here. Why did he ever start across this ice mirror. At this altitude, you've got to rest. Can't rest out here. Bullshit. Left foot now. Hammer. Axe. Left foot. Right foot. Axe. Hammer. Ice axe. Pick. Crampon points. Time without end. A dull repetition without end. Wrong. Everything ends.

The ice crab cometh. He was almost there. 200 meters in half an hour, or was it two hours? He didn't know. But suddenly he knew he only had half a dozen steep steps to go and now, the angle was slacking off, steep ice giving way to less steep ice, finally to less steep snow. And then, instead of swinging the pick of his axe into the ice in front of his face, he was pushing the shaft of the axe down into the snow, the welcoming snow, a flattening sweep of snow, leading out to an even flatter hump on a big ridge.

A few more steps. A few more. Just a few. Then no more.

4

—*Do something, chrissakes, do something!...*
—*Why?*
—*Just do something, keep moving, you're still too high, stay up here and you'll freeze to death. You don't want to freeze do you?*
—*Dunno.... don't think so.... Why?*

Too many unanswered questions. Always had been. *Why? Too many whys.*

Never could explain it, to anyone, not to Nicole, not to his brothers, his parents. his friends, his other friends, who were they? were they really his friends? And explain what, exactly? Who he was, what he was doing, what he was planning to do, and why, and why not? Just do it.

—*That's the answer Miles, just do it. Something. Anything. Just move, don't stop now.*

Miles is sitting in the snow, it's lower-angle snow now. After tiptoeing across the ice cliff, he's moved on, across a dozen more meters of friendly, flattening out snow, to the beginning of a new ridge, or a new part of the same ridge, twisting down from the summit of Gyangtse II, a new place. A safe place. And without really deciding to, he just sits down, stunned, still out of breath. Surprised to be here. Surprised he's made it this far. Surprised to be alive. Sitting, head on his arms, arms on his knees. Trying to think. Not really succeeding.

If I keep going I'll feel better, bound to. Every few hundred meters lower there'll be more air to breathe, gotta feel better.... C'mon.... try.

He tries, moves, stands back up, starts walking. Down the ridge. Again.

Yeah, walking. This isn't climbing, he thought, just walking. Walking down a steep ridge. But it can't last....

It does. It lasts. For a while. Time stops. His steps, the ticking of a metronome. His breathing, easier now, another rhythm, a different metronome. The crunch of crampon points into wind-blasted snow: step-step, crunch-crunch, step-step, breath-breath, and repeat, now and forever, step-step, crunch-crunch.

The panorama below him, in front of him, down there: a crazy wide-angle confusion of clouds and ice. Cloud wisps, tendrils of mist, curl up from what must be a glacial basin down there, down below. Afternoon sunlight throws twisting thin cloud shadows onto thicker cloud blankets. Cloud shapes fight with cloud shadows. Miles looks away, almost dizzy. Looks at the ridge in front of him, moving past him in slow motion, as he steps, lurches, walks in slow motion down the slope that isn't a slope but only a rounded spine of snow, slowly steepening, gently steeper every few steps, slightly narrower now, and narrower still every few steps, every few minutes. Miles can't tell them apart, the minutes, the steps, but something is changing. And yes, he is breathing easier now, at least imagines he is breathing easier, not well but better. But he isn't really walking better, he is tired, bone weary. And his mind is wandering, his eyes too, away from the snow in front of him, and back left and down to the confused space beneath him. The ridge curving slowly around to the left, rimming a sort of giant bowl, and at the bottom somewhere under all those clouds, maybe a way out, an exit, down toward the Tibetan plateau. Maybe, maybe not....

The ridge, the climb up, the climb down, climbing, walking, staggering, it all blurs into one big maybe. Maybe I can do it. Maybe I can't. For sure I can't if I can't concentrate, concentrate more than this. Stop daydreaming. Pay attention. He is talking to himself now, but that's another distraction, looking around, looking down, instead of right ahead at the next few meters of white reality: snow or ice? which is it? And what comes next. He can't help himself, his bloodshot stinging eyes scanning this wide steep basin, too steep to call it a bowl, a kind of cirque maybe not too bad, not too steep, funneling down, down, down to a kind of mid-mountain shelf where the north side of Gyangtse II takes a break, pauses its dizzy descent, toward the Tibetan plateau, now almost invisible under rising, boiling, afternoon clouds. Maybe if I could see a little farther, lower down, through these clouds, maybe I could figure out the best way down. Zigzag back and forth down this snow funnel, or turn in and front point backward—what a pain, what a hassle, what the—what the—

O ... My ... God ... Omygod, Omygod. The whole slow-motion disaster unfolding in a second that lasts forever, impossible to stop, impossible to rewind. Miles' left foot swinging forward, mechanically, innocently, the sharp front points of his crampon catching the red nylon of his wind pants. DAMN. Damn Damn damn.... Silent curses, as he feels himself tilt in space, tilt forward, unable to react in time, unable to jam his ice axe into the snow, as he turns slowly upside down, as he falls, falls, falls....

5

Snow ... sky ... snow ... sky ... spinning by ... tumbling one over the other. No, the sky wasn't tumbling, he was tumbling, tumbling and fumbling to get a grip on his ice axe with both hands, self arrest, slow down, stop ... It wasn't happening. It wasn't going to happen. Falling. Just falling.

It was a long way down, and he was going all the way down. Down this steep face, this slightly hollow concave face of snow. And somewhere down there it would flatten out at the top of a Chinese glacier twisting up from an imaginary place called Tibet. He wasn't thinking of Tibet, he wasn't thinking at all, he was falling, sliding, then catching a crampon in the snow and tumbling again, hurting, halfway between surprised and numb. Just falling. And it was taking forever.

It took maybe two minutes. Maybe as much as a thousand meters. He came to a stop. A full stop.

Quiet. It was quiet. Not a sound.

And he was still alive.

His voice croaked, caught: *still ... alive ...*

Alive but damaged, hurt and hurting. One big difference: he could feel it already, he could breathe. Must be a long way farther down, in thicker air now. And the other difference: his arm, his left arm, hurt more than everything else, wasn't moving, didn't want to move.

Miles lay half on his side, crumpled up, or so it felt. He had to get up, or did he? Really?

He opened his eyes. Blinked. reached up with his right hand to straighten his glacier glasses: still dark, sure the glasses were dark, but the world, the snow all around him seemed darker. Was darker. How late was it now? Plenty late. How much more daylight? He didn't care, at least part of him didn't care. He closed his eyes again, drifted off into the darkness...

still ... alive ... still ... alive. The words echoed softly through a kind of twilight haze, the music was familiar, it filled the dark space. He'd heard it a thousand times, and with an effort he remembered what it was: Berlioz, *Lélio ou le retour à la vie.* Now the voice was French, it wasn't Nicole's voice but an off-stage voice, breathy: "*Dieu, je vis encore....*" The music was already fading, the voice too: "*Dieu, je vis encore....*"

Waking up, like Lélio, from a bad dream, a bad trip, no just from a bad fall. Knocked him out cold. For how long? Knocked the stuffing out of him. That's crazy, what stuffing? *I'm hallucinating, been hallucinating for a long time, but the pain is real, my left arm is real.... Hurts like Hell.* He is sitting up now, he doesn't even know how he managed to sit up, how he managed to survive the fall. He is a mass of aches, but his left arm, his left shoulder is the biggest ache of all, bigger than he is, bigger than this damn mountain, too big to deal with. Miles wants to close his eyes and listen to the music. Somehow he doesn't. Time to go. At least to stand up. Or try to stand up. And then make a sling for his left arm with a loop of nylon webbing. Lifting his arm, he almost screamed but the sound didn't get past his cracked lips. And then with his arm supported across his chest, the pain started to fade, a little, then a little more, just enough to move.

Miles looked around, looked out, out and down, north toward Tibet, in the gathering twilight. Across a kind of plateau of snow, a shelf breaking the steady dropping slope of the mountain. White on white, no shadows, white on white turning quickly to a soft gray on gray, dimming, featureless. He gazed up at the crest of that ridge, so far above, where he'd been, where his fall had begun, shook his head, turned his back on Gyangtse II and started walking north. Yeah, breathing was easier, walking wasn't. The snow wasn't deep, but he could hardly lift his boots and swing each one forward, foot after foot after foot. Inching across this big shelf of snow. Miles knew it was really a hanging glacier, a big flat cake with a smooth frosting of fresh white snow. Ahead of him, in the fading light, it would drop over another edge, another change in the slope, and it would buckle. The smooth surface of the snow would start to crack and split, crevasses would open their blue mouths even though now it was too dark to see the blue, just shadows.

The first shadows, soft shadows, gentle folds across the slope, were starting to appear in the snow in front of him. If he simply stumbled forward, soon one of those shadows would turn into a real crevasse, a real crevasse whose snowy cover would not be strong enough to support his weight. The story, his story, would be over. An irregular drunken line of footprints in the snow, leading to a dark hole.

—*Miles, Look out! you can get around to the right!*

—*What?*

—*Pay attention! Go right!* He was paying attention now. A bit late he thought. And he walked to the right, around an obvious fold in the snow, that was an obvious crevasse. And he was thinking hard, almost clearly, almost.

I'm going to spend the night out here. Still too high. It's going to be too cold. Too damn cold. I'll be a lump of ice in the morning. Well, no, that's just a manner of speaking, a way of talking. And who the hell am I talking to? Myself? Who's talking to me? Myself?

—You know better.
—I don't know anything.
—Start looking. Find something, somewhere to shelter.
—Like what?
—Like that crevasse, over there....

Falling light, rising wind, a scrim of windblown powder moving over the surface of the snow, hard to see even the obvious, and here in this evening grayness, on an almost featureless glacial shelf on an unknown face of a little known mountain nothing was obvious. Miles started to walk forward, stepped carefully forward, looking for the next crevasse. He didn't find it. It found him.

6

Not again! Oh shit, not again!

Too tired even to swear, to open his mouth, he feels the snow around him begin to crumble, to sink, subside, break into chunks. He feels himself dropping, slowly, cushioned by the collapsing snow. Part of him has already given up, now the rest of him lets go. Part of him is watching as he sinks in a cloud of snow into this half-filled crevasse. Part of him is waiting for the long drop into a narrow, blue, icy vice, for the two walls of this crack in the glacier to squeeze him tight, to end his fall, end his story, end his life. He's waiting and it doesn't happen. Miles falls maybe 8 meters, 10 meters, and stops, covered with chunks of snow, onto something, down below the surface of the glacier, something that feels like a snowy floor. That's what it is. The crevasse is filled up right here, by a sort of snow bridge, solid enough to stop his fall. Another close one, way too close. Miles is shaking—the violent physical exhaustion of survival, too much, too damn much, too much to understand, too much really to even believe. He doesn't move, doesn't want to move, doesn't want to disturb the stability of this false floor in a larger crevasse that might not be strong enough, that might still collapse and swallow him.

He shakes and shivers, not from the cold. Clutches his injured arm to his chest. Realizes that he hasn't dropped his ice axe, it's still fastened to his wrist even though it's so dark now, that he can't see it. Realizes that he can't, won't, shouldn't, do anything at all. Just wait, if he can, wait for morning, for tomorrow, for answers to questions he doesn't dare ask, not yet.

Maybe tomorrow, if there is a tomorrow. He closes his eyes, it is still just as dark.

7

Nicole was there waiting for him when he climbed out of the crevasse. She always waited for him. What a gal! What had he done to deserve her? How come she put up with him, stuck around, was always waiting for him when he got back from those crazy climbs? Hank and Peter were there too. No way. Not possible. He'd last seen them way down below him, half way up their south face route, moving slow but still moving, climbing up after him, even though they weren't strong enough to catch up, hadn't been ready for that predawn start. Well, to tell the truth he hadn't been ready either, but he did it, made himself do it. Got out of the tent, tightened his crampons and left the two of them there, sleeping. He knew they weren't up to it. Wasn't his fault. Was it? Looking back down, hours later, at what had been their route, spotting that new avalanche track that had pretty well wiped the route clean, and must have wiped them clean off the route, re-contoured that curving rib they had always counted on to reach the upper slopes and the final ridge. And now, no one in sight. The two of them gone. Just gone. Why had they followed him? Why hadn't it avalanched earlier when he was steaming up that same stretch of the route? when he was fresh, before the altitude and the difficult climbing finally got him? Why? Why? Too many questions? Too few answers. But here they were, Hank and Peter, grinning, and opening a bottle of wine. No, that was Nicole, pulling a green bottle out of her day pack, *un petit Muscadet*, her favorite white wine, perfect for an afternoon picnic after a good day bouldering on one of the tougher circuits in the *forêt de Fontainebleau*. Nicole was laughing, that wonderful high-pitched laugher—how can laughter have such a French accent?—and the boys were laughing too, especially Peter, cracking up at a joke he hadn't heard, a private joke? and now he had to join in, he was laughing too, laughing until it hurt. And it really hurt.

Everything hurt. Waking up hurt. Sunlight filtering down through the torn gap in the snowy roof of his crevasse hurt his eyes, his shoulder hurt, the stiff fingers of his hands hurt, the memory of climbing down from the summit of Gyangtse II made him feel sick, nauseous. He wasn't ready for a new day, anything but, but had no choice. Crooked and cramped in a tumbled pile of snow blocks, where he'd spent the night, afraid to move. More passed out than asleep. Miles shook himself, shook his good arm, decided he could move, could even stand up if he had to. He had to. And he did. Looked around and looked up. Movement was a good drug, It helped, it always had. But how was he going to move, and where?

The crevasse wasn't very wide, which is probably why falling and drifting snow had been able to block it, block it and stop Miles' fall. The blue crevasse walls weren't exactly parallel either. The whole crevasse seemed to get narrower off to his right. Maybe narrow enough that he could try to chimney his way up and out, putting his back against one wall and his feet with their stick-to-the-ice crampon points on the other. A classical maneuver, easy on rock, less so on ice, even less so with one good arm. But his ice axe might help. Let's see....

—Hey down there, you okay?

—Who's that? Who's there?

—Never mind, just tie on.... We'll give you some tension, a tight rope.

There was no tight rope. There was no rope.

So maybe I can pull up on the pick of my axe with one arm. Hold my position, put one foot behind me, make another move. Move my other foot.

Put the axe in again. Chimney out of here.
—*Keep it up, you're getting closer.*

Getting nowhere, too slow, too lame, taking forever for each move. Stopping, coughing, sweating, then moving again. Almost up to that ragged hole in the icy ceiling of the crevasse. Light sneaking in from above. And now the hardest part, getting out, over this lip, almost an overhang. Hell, he'd done this a hundred times back in Colorado, exiting ice climbs onto crumbly snow faces. And here the ice was giving way to pretty solid snow, almost solid, almost good enough to jam that axe in one more time, one more time.

—*C'mon, I'll give you a hand.*

He was out, scrambling on hands and knees, no, on one hand and two knees, shaking, and shaking his head in disbelief.

How'd I do that? Who the hell helped me over that lip? There's sure as hell nobody here. Never was.... even though I heard.... who? Who cares? I'm out.

8

A new day on the flank of a new mountain—one he has never seen before. But it's the same mountain, the same death trap of a mountain, even though now he is so much lower. A new chapter in a story he still doesn't understand, a story that could have ended a dozen times, but didn't, and still could any moment.

Miles squints, pushes his glacier glasses back straight on his face, looks around. Looks for answers that aren't there. But he is, against all odds he thinks, and realizes, yes, that he is actually thinking now, thinking better, more oxygen, less wind, thinking in complete sentences it seems, or something similar, complete thoughts anyway.

Not just thinking about what to do next, or whether to do anything. Thinking, or starting to think, about why he's here, why he climbed this damn peak, why he left his buddies in camp, why he left Nicole in Paris, why he finally started down the back side when he didn't even know if he could, wasn't sure he wanted to, wasn't sure why, and still isn't. That much is for sure. His mind is buzzing with questions. But there are no answers. Maybe down there, at the bottom of this last, long, sloping, winding glacier he'll find some answers. Not necessarily the ones he is looking for. But some answers, to some questions. Down there, off the mountain, in those arid Tibetan highlands, in those dark Tibetan faces he's only seen in books, magazines, never yet in person, high herdsmen, nomads he won't even be able to talk to.... if he ever gets that far. Wondering about how many more half-hidden crevasses are waiting, invisibly waiting, in this last tail end of the glacier, on this last white highway to the base of the peak, the other base on this other side of his peak.

Miles is thinking that if he could only ask the right questions, he might find the right answers. The morning sunshine is tickling him now, still cold but not impossibly cold, still hurting but not terminally hurting, still looking down the mountain, down this long glacier. There is still only one direction that matters: down. The glacier he's standing on stretches off into the morning haze, small wisps of cloud already rising from the valleys beneath. The lower he goes, the less snow cover he'll find on the snow bridges over more crevasses, lots more crevasses. Will he see them? Will those damn voices warn him before he crashes through the surface snow again? No rope mates to check the fall, pull him out again. But somewhere down there he knows he is waiting for himself. His life is waiting for him to grab it, to start over, and keep going. And somewhere up there, behind him, up on the mountain, he thinks, maybe he found an answer, not the answer but an answer, anyway. Maybe the answer was just moving, climbing down just as important as climbing up, just moving. Is that all you have to do? Or moving toward something. Toward other people, other stories. He still doesn't know. There are a lot of maybes, lots of ifs. Maybe if he starts walking on down the glacier he'll actually reach the foot of the peak, rock, scree, dirt, life. Or maybe another crevasse will bring this story to an end. He doesn't know, he can't know. But he feels ready. The glacier is waiting. The morning is waiting. No more waiting.

Miles hitches up his painful arm in its improvised sling, grabs his ice axe with his right hand, starts walking....

Early days in the Valley ....

About the Author

LITO TEJADA-FLORES was captured by mountains, seduced by climbing, at an early age. Born at 13,000 feet in La Paz, Bolivia, he grew up in southern California dreaming about being somewhere else. He started rock climbing on a Sierra Club outing at the age of 13, and that somewhere else turned out to be the granite cliffs of Tahquitz Rock and later Yosemite Valley. Climbing was intoxicating, made more sense than anything else, more than school, or looking for a career, or making money. Climbing opened a lot of doors, took Lito around the world, introduced him to the best friends and companions anyone could have. Cliffs morphed into peaks, summers on the crags blended smoothly into winters on skis, and scribbled notes in the summit registers of his teenage climbs across the Sierra Nevada slowly grew into stories that began to be published in the few climbing journals of the 60s and 70s. Eventually climbing writing led to climbing publishing, and a long collaboration with Al Steck and Steve Roper, editing *Ascent* magazine. Lito is still mad about mountains, splitting his year between the Sangre de Cristo range of the Colorado Rockies, and the southern Andes of Chilean Patagonia, with his wife and partner, wilderness photographer Linde Waidhofer.

Lito would love to hear from you, and you can write him at litotf@westerneye.com

Photo Credits

Front cover, Chris Jones,
    La Catedral, Bariloche, Argentina.
Fontespiece, Edgar Boyles,
    Chouinard-Herbert route, Sentinel rock, Yosemite

p 2   Bouldering, the purest game
p 14   Direct west face of the Aguille du Dru, Chamonix
p 20   Chris Jones, La Catedral, Bariloche, Argentina
p 26   Hans Bruning, The Devils Thumb, SE Alaska
p 50   Edgar Boyles, Cado Avenali in action
p 54   National Park Service photo, Grand Teton & Mt. Owen
p 64   Chris Jones, Lito filming on Fitz Roy
p 68   Linde Waidhofer, Monte Fitz Roy
p 74   Linde Waidhofer, Cerro Torre
p 84   Linde Waidhofer, endless peaks
p 108 Edgar Boyles, early aid climbing, Yosemite

For the life of me I can't remember who made the graphic bouldering photo on page 2; nor am I sure who took the photo of me on the West Face of the Dru on page 14, during an early attempt with John Harlin. But thank you nonetheless to all my photographer friends.

www.ingramcontent.com/pod-product-compliance
Lightning Source LLC
Chambersburg PA
CBHW071712040426
42446CB00011B/2028